PAINTING
songbirds

with Sherry C. Nelson

by Sherry C. Nelson

PAINTING
songbirds
with Sherry C. Nelson

NORTH LIGHT BOOKS
CINCINNATI, OHIO
www.artistsnetwork.com

Published by North Light Books, an imprint of F+W Publications, Inc., 4700 E. Galbraith Road, Cincinnati, Ohio, 45236. (800) 289-0963. First Edition.

Other fine North Light Books are available from your local bookstore, art supply store or direct from the publisher.

11 10 09 08 07   5 4 3 2 1

Distributed In Canada By Fraser Direct, 100 Armstrong Avenue, Georgetown, ON, Canada L7G 5S4, Tel: (905) 877-4411

Distributed in the U.K. and Europe by David & Charles, Brunel House, Newton Abbot, Devon, TQ12 4PU, England, Tel: (+44) 1626 323200, Fax: (+44) 1626 323319, Email: postmaster@davidandcharles.co.uk

Distributed in Australia by Capricorn Link, P.O. Box 704, S. Windsor NSW, 2756 Australia, Tel: (02) 4577-3555

Library of Congress Cataloging-in-Publication Data

Nelson, Sherry C.

   Painting songbirds with Sherry C. Nelson / Sherry C. Nelson.

      p. cm.

   Includes index.

   ISBN-13: 978-1-58180-877-3 (hardcover : alk. paper)

   ISBN-10: 1-58180-877-1 (hardcover : alk. paper)

   ISBN-13: 978-1-58180-876-6 (pbk. : alk. paper)

   ISBN-10: 1-58180-876-3 (pbk. : alk. paper)

  1. Songbirds in art. 2. Painting--Technique. I. Nelson, Sherry C.

  II. Title.

ND1380.N452 2007

751.45'43288--dc22

                              2006022866

Edited by Kathy Kipp
Designed by Clare Finney
Interior layout by Kathy Gardner
Production coordinated by Greg Nock

Photographs on pages 83, 91, 99, 107, 131 and 139 used by permission of Terry R. Steele.
Photographs on pages 35, 51, 59, 75, 99 and 115 used by permission of Arthur Morris (www.birdsasart.com)
All step-by-step and other reference photography by Deborah Anne Galloway.

METRIC CONVERSION CHART

To convert	to	multiply by
Inches	Centimeters	2.54
Centimeters	Inches	0.4
Feet	Centimeters	30.5
Centimeters	Feet	0.03
Yards	Meters	0.9
Meters	Yards	1.1

ABOUT THE AUTHOR

Sherry Nelson's career in painting has stretched across nearly 36 years, and has been shaped by her love of the natural world and its creatures. First and foremost she is a teacher, and has shared her wildlife painting techniques with thousands of students in every single state and many countries around the world.

If painting and teaching is her career and first love, then field work is Sherry's obsession. Travel teaching has provided an unparalleled opportunity to see the birds and animals of the world along with her students. Sherry is an accomplished naturalist, and shares her love of birds and animals as well as painting with her students. She claims that field study is so addictive that it's sometimes tempting to forsake brush for binoculars. And it's the field work that brings realism to the birds and animals she paints, endowing each species with the special characteristics that make it look real. It's easy to see that Sherry is on speaking terms with the creatures she paints.

Sherry has developed a unique approach to teaching, breaking down the instructions into a step-by-step sequence that allows almost anyone to learn quickly and easily master the techniques needed to produce beautiful and realistic animals, flowers and birds.

Sherry was born in Alton, Illinois, and received her B.A. from Southern Illinois University. The lure of the mountains of the Southwest prompted a move to New Mexico, where her children, Neil and Berit, were raised. Sherry now lives and paints on her 37 acres of spectacular wilderness in the Chiricahua Mountains of Southeast Arizona. Nine species of hummingbirds and the occasional black bear frequent the feeders, and the coatis and gray foxes come by frequently for hand-outs. Now, from her studio in wooded Cave Creek Canyon, Sherry invites you to join her in painting some of your favorite songbirds.

DEDICATION

To my son Neil Nelson, and my daughter Berit Nelson. Since childhood, you both have shown a great appreciation for your Mom's painting, even when countless classes and travel teaching complicated your lives. Now, as adults, it gives me great satisfaction to know that you continue to love my work, and enjoy so many of my paintings in your homes. Thank you both for your support and enthusiasm along the way.

ACKNOWLEDGMENTS

As always, much appreciation is due to Deborah A. Galloway, my business partner and friend of many years. Deby shot all the step-by-step photos for this book, provided many of the reference shots I used for the designs, and helped me in countless ways through the many steps and hours of work that goes into a book such as this. Without her, this book would not be in your hands. And without her, I could not do what I do. Thanks, Deb, one more time!

Many thanks to my good friends Terry Steele and Arthur Morris. Professional wildlife photographers, they share their "seconds" with me, giving me a world of fresh inspiration. Your generosity provides a valuable and priceless bounty of reference material that encourages me to keep designing and painting.

And to my editor at North Light Books: Thanks in abundance to Kathy Kipp, who makes it all come together. Kathy is incredibly skilled at bringing out the best in her authors, and I cannot thank her enough for her help, her talent, her limitless patience and most of all, her friendship through the birth of another book. Thanks also to others on my North Light team, who each bring their own special skills to bear in making a beautiful book come to life: Clare Finney, who designed the cover and the interior, and Greg Nock, the production coordinator who shepherded this book through the printing process.

Table of Contents

15 STEP-BY-STEP DEMONSTRATIONS

These are organized in approximate order of difficulty. Beginning bird painters should start with the first few demos.

Materials

For this entire book, I've used only ten different tubes of paint! I've limited what you'll need, so you can afford to buy the best. I use Winsor & Newton Artists' Oil Colours. They last a long time since you need only a small amount for a project. Buying inexpensive paints is not a savings; they are mostly oil and very little pigment.

Buy the best brushes you can afford. If you attempt these projects with poor quality brushes, you may blame yourself if your paintings don't turn out right. Using good quality red sable short brights will make the techniques work for you.

If you've painted in oils before, you may have some of the supplies you need. If not, just purchase what you need for your favorite projects from this book to minimize expense. But always buy the very best you can afford. That's your best guarantee for success.

BASIC SUPPLIES

Listed here are the painting supplies you will need for every project in this book.

- **Palette Pad:** A 9 x 12-inch (22.9cm x 30.5cm) strip palette for oils is best.

- **Palette Knife:** A flat painting knife is best for mixing in the cobalt drier with your oils.

- **Cobalt Drier:** This product is optional, but I encourage you to try it. When used as I do, your painting will dry overnight, yet it leaves the palette workable until you are finished with the painting.

- **Brushes:** Red sable short brights in size nos. 0, 2, 4, 6 and 8. Also a red sable round liner brush in size no. 0.

- **Artist's Odorless Thinner:** You need a tiny capped jar to pour a little into when you paint. I use a small empty lip balm jar and I keep it capped until I need it.

- **Turpenoid Natural:** A non-toxic, oily brush cleaner and medium for oils.

- **Masonite or hardboard panels** in the sizes suggested for each project. You can purchase large sheets and cut it yourself or have it cut at a home center.

- **Dark gray artist's graphite paper** for transferring the designs. Purchase at an art supply store in a large sheet, not in a roll from a craft store. Craft papers may be hard to remove from the surface and may not be thinner soluble.

- **Tracing Paper:** A 9 x 12-inch (22.9cm x 30.5cm) pad.

- **Stylus:** You can also use an old ballpoint pen for marking feather lines into the wet paint.

- **Ballpoint Pen:** Not a pencil, for transferring the designs.

- **Paper Towels:** Soft and very smooth. Viva are best, and will save lots of wear and tear on your brushes. Don't use the cheap, bumpy ones.

- **Spray Varnish:** Final finish for the completed paintings.

- **Artgel:** This Winsor & Newton product cleans oil brushes and works well for removing oil paint from clothing and hands.

BACKGROUND PREPARATION

If you've not painted before, you may wish to simplify your background preparation and concentrate on learning the basic painting skills. For example, any project in this book may be painted on just a single neutral acrylic color. As you complete more projects, you may wish to purchase some or all of the acrylic colors I used, which are shown on page 11.

Here is what you will need to prepare your backgrounds as I did for the projects in this book:

• **Masonite or hardboard panel:** To paint on.

• **Sponge Roller:** I apply all background colors with these 2-inch (51mm) foam rollers. They give an even, slightly textured surface for painting.

• **Acrylic Retarder:** This slows the drying time of acrylic paints. I use Jo Sonja's Retarder Medium.

• **320-Grit Wet/Dry Sandpaper:** It's black and available in packs at home centers or lumberyards.

• **Liberty Matte Finish:** A must. This acrylic matte spray will seal the surface of the background lightly, allowing the oil paints to move easily for blending. (NOTE: I formerly used Krylon Matte Finish to seal the backgrounds before painting. That product's formulation has been changed and it can no longer be used for this purpose.)

• **Newspaper:** To protect your work surface.

• **Paper Towels:** These can be the less expensive ones, since they'll just be used for clean-up.

Materials
AT A GLANCE

Try to avoid substitutions. Use materials as close as possible to the ones I use for the best results.

• **Oil Paint:** Winsor & Newton Artists' Oils. They are the best and only oil paints that I use.

• **Brushes:** Sherry C. Nelson Series 303 red sable short brights, nos. 0, 2, 4, 6 and 8. Sherry C. Nelson Series 312 red sable mix rounds, nos. 0 and 1.

• **Palette Knife:** I use a flat-bladed painting knife styled after the Italian painting knives. It's best for mixing in drier and keeps my hand out of the paint.

• **Cobalt Drier:** by Grumbacher.

• **Delta Ceramcoat Acrylic Paints:** Light Ivory, Old Parchment, Flesh Tan, Butter Yellow, Trail Tan, Desert Sun Orange, Moss Green, Seminole Green, Gamal Green, Tide Pool Blue, Williamsburg Blue, Cayenne, Antique Rose.

• **Spray Finishes:** Liberty Matte Finish, by Liberty Finishes. For ordering information, see www.sherrycnelson.com.

• **Krylon Spray Varnish:** #7002, for final picture varnish.

SUPPLY RESOURCE

If you have problems locating what you need in your local stores, you may purchase supplies by mail order from:

The Magic Brush, Inc.
P.O. Box 16530
Portal, AZ 85632

Phone or fax: (520) 558-2285.
www.sherrycnelson.com
orders@sherrycnelson.com

Send $3.00 U.S. to receive a catalog.

Sherry's Top Ten Oil Colors

I used my Top Ten favorite Winsor & Newton Artists' Oils for all the projects in this book. That's right, all 15 projects are painted with just these ten colors!

This is my palette set-up, too. I put the most frequently used colors in the bottom row on my palette closest to me, and the less-used further away. That way I don't have to keep reaching to get to the colors I use the most!

Sap Green   Cadmium Yellow Pale   Winsor Red   Alizarin Crimson   French Ultramarine

Ivory Black   Titanium White   Raw Sienna   Raw Umber   Burnt Sienna

Acrylic Colors for Background Preparation

These are the colors of acrylic paint I used to paint the backgrounds on all the projects in this book. They're made by Delta Ceramcoat and are available at most craft supply stores in handy 2-oz. (59ml) squeeze bottles.

If you prefer another brand, these samples will help you find the closest color match. See pages 12 and 13 for complete step-by-step instructions on painting the backgrounds.

Light Ivory

Old Parchment

Flesh Tan

Butter Yellow

Trail Tan

Desert Sun Orange

Moss Green

Seminole Green

Gamal Green

Tide Pool Blue

Williamsburg Blue

Cayenne

Antique Rose

Preparing the Backgrounds

The background can make or break the look of the finished art, depending on how well it's prepared. Set up a worktable and have everything you need nearby. You'll do a better job if you don't have to hunt for something after you begin.

Did you ever notice the beautiful out-of-focus backgrounds in many animal and bird photos? The animal is in focus and the background, usually foliage with light and dark areas, is soft and hazy and gives special emphasis to the creature in the photo. I have adapted my background treatments to incorporate that impression.

A background should stay in the background. It shouldn't be so complex or colorful that it detracts from your subject. Simplicity and neutral colors will allow your design to be focal. If your background gets too gaudy, you probably won't like the finished painting.

All the backgrounds used in this book are done with the wet-on-wet acrylic method I'm going to demonstrate here. And please, don't be intimidated. What's the worst-case scenario? If you don't like what you get, just let it dry, sand it and try again!

Before beginning, reconstitute the acrylic paint. For new bottles, unscrew the lid, fill with water to the bottom of the neck, recap and shake well. For used bottles, add a little water and shake, until it has the same "liquid" sound.

Sand the edges of the masonite panel; do not sand the painting surface. If the back is fuzzy, sand that too, so the particles don't get into your paint. I do the backs with a small electric sander, out of doors.

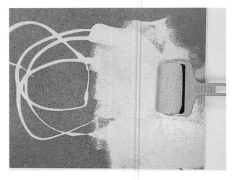

1. The wet-on-wet acrylic backgrounds used in this book all begin with a basecoat of one of the colors. Here I've drizzled on Moss Green, quite generously. You'll need enough to wet the roller as well as to coat the surface liberally. How do you know when too much is too much? If the paint remains bubbly after you've coated the entire surface, you've put on a little too much. If it's sticky, and disappears right away into the surface, too little. Use the sponge roller in one direction until the surface is covered. Then go across in the other direction for a smoother finish. Lighten the pressure on the roller when you change directions. If you've put on too much paint, just change directions another time. The paint will gradually quit being bubbly.

2. After the first coat dries (it will no longer feel cool to the touch), sand it well. Sand the edges again and the painting surface too, to remove any "cruddies" that may have gotten into the paint. Press lightly on the sandpaper and move it around on the surface as if you were polishing it.

Sherry C. Nelson

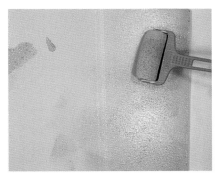

3. Recoat the surface with Moss Green and roll evenly over the surface, using a little less than before and working more quickly, since the other colors must be applied while the surface is wet. Now add the shading color, Tide Pool Blue. I placed two drizzles of it on the surface, and rolled lengthwise into them, not across the stripe. I'm moving the roller around a bit as I work, to distribute the blue, and to blend it into the background.

4. Now add the Light Ivory in a different place and reblend in the same manner. If you feel you can't control a color easily, roll some off on a paper towel or on the newspaper. Here I've worked the Ivory into the upper left part of the surface to highlight, and I've left the colors just a little splotchy. Remember, we're wanting out-of-focus here.

5. Were you able to get the last of the blending done before the colors dried? If not, you can add a squirt of acrylic retarder on the surface as you basecoat the second time. That will make it easier to finish all blending before the paint begins to dry, so that the acrylic has time to settle onto the surface, to flatten out. If your backgrounds are too bumpy and they dry too quickly, use more paint, use a little retarder and work faster! Sand well until the surface is smooth. Resand edges, too, and wipe off sanding dust.

6. Take the surface outside, preferably on a windless, warm, sunny day and shake the can of Liberty Matte Finish well. Hold the can about a foot from the surface and begin spraying at the top. Working from side to side, let the spray go off the edge before starting back across in order to prevent pileup. Hold the surface to the light so you can see the spray fall, and move on as you see it beginning to coat the surface. Spray one light, even coat. You'll soon learn how much is too little (the oils won't blend easily) or too much (when the oils slide around too readily). Let dry outside for 15 minutes before bringing it indoors.

Final Finish

Not all oil paints dry with an even finish. Some, like the reds and umbers, become dull. Others look wet even when they are dry. To give the surface of a painting a uniform sheen, it is necessary to apply a final finish. The finish also protects the paint.

When cobalt drier is used to speed the drying time of your palette, it also shortens the time you must wait before you can apply the final varnish. The thickness of the paint you've applied to the painting also impacts the drying time. Obviously the thicker the paint, the longer you have to wait for the paint to cure and be safe to varnish. Remember: Just because the paint is dry to the touch does not mean it is ready for the final finish.

Since my painting style involves only the thinnest of paint applications and since I live in a warm dry climate, I can probably varnish sooner than those of you hampered by cold weather and lots of humidity.

Generally, I feel safe varnishing my paintings by the second week, though I've done it sooner with no problem. I'll leave that decision to you. I use Krylon Spray Varnish, #7002. It is a satin finish, oil-based varnish that gives a very light, even coating and brings out the beautiful rich colors for which oils are noted. I've never experienced crazing or other varnish-related problems.

Transferring the Design

For each of the projects in this book, there is a line drawing to make it easier for you to begin painting. Because accuracy is so essential for making your bird paintings realistic, if at all possible, transfer the design from a photocopy of the line drawing, not a traced copy.

If you cannot make a photocopy of the design, you will have to trace it. Make as exact a copy as possible; every deviation from the line drawing will impact the final appearance of your painting.

Use artist's graphite, sold in large sheets in art supply stores, for transferring. It is important to use graphite that is thinner soluble, so you can come back later and clean off the excess graphite. I'll show you how in Step 3 below.

 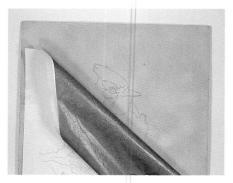

1. Lay a piece of dark graphite on top of the prepared background. Lay the line drawing on top of the graphite and position it as you desire. Tape one edge of the line drawing, not the graphite paper, to the painting surface.

Now lay a piece of tracing paper over the design and tape it if you wish. Begin making the transfer, using a ballpoint pen. Check the painting surface after you've drawn a few lines. Is the transfer too light or too dark? Adjust the pressure to get it just right.

Use a ballpoint pen; do not use a pencil, which tends to make less accurate lines as the point wears down. Carefully transfer all detail included in the line drawing. I even transfer spots and other pattern areas so they will show through my sparse basecoat later. The tracing paper is essential to help you determine if you've skipped any areas, and it will protect your line drawing for another use.

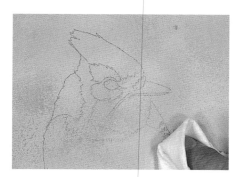

2. On light backgrounds, or when using brand new graphite paper, the transfer is sometimes too dark. Fold a dry paper towel into a pad, and use it to soften the transfer. You can pick up most of the excess graphite this way; be careful not to remove too much.

It particularly helps to remove excess graphite in this manner when you are painting a pale flower, for example, on a light background, when too-heavy graphite would be hard to cover and white graphite would not be easily visible.

3. When you've completed the design, you can remove any graphite that still shows around design edges. Dip the no. 8 bright into odorless thinner. Blot the brush well on a paper towel. Work the brush along the edge to lift up the graphite line. As you can see, it's very important to have graphite that is thinner soluble. You'll never have to worry about removing graphite lines that could show underneath your sparse basecoats; they simply dissolve in the paint as you blend, in a way that water-soluble graphite, made for use with acrylics, won't do.

A brush dampened with thinner can also be used like an eraser as you are painting. You can lift out small areas of paint, clean up along edges and remove mistakes entirely, if need be. Just remember to dip, then blot. If you leave thinner in the brush, it will bleed out into the painting as soon as the brush touches the surface.

Setting Up the Palette

Not all disposable palettes are equal. Make sure the palette you buy is oil-impervious. If you put out paint and an hour later discover an oil ring around each color, the palette is NOT impervious to oil and will ruin your paints by soaking most of the oil out of them. You'll also have the choice between a wax and a matte surface. Either will do a good job.

Do not tear off a single sheet to put the paint on. Leave the sheets attached to the palette so the whole thing doesn't slide around as you work. Fold two or three paper towels in quarters and stack the folded ends under the edge of the palette pad. That way you'll have a flat surface to dry wipe the brush on, folds to slide the brush between to squeeze dry, and the palette will hold them down.

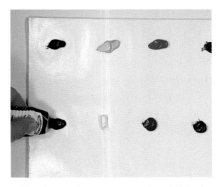

1. Here's how I put out my paint: 1/4-inch (6mm) of paint from the tube of each color is plenty. I lay the colors out in two rows, the most used black, white and earth colors on the bottom row, closest to me, and the least used reds, greens and yellows in the top row, furthest from my hand.

Leave space between them for mixing the drier into the paint, and for making loading zones and mixes with the different colors.

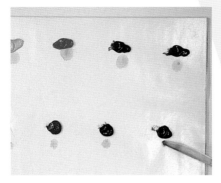

2. Dip the palette knife into the drier and bleed excess off the knife on the side of the bottle. Immediately recap the bottle to keep it from drying out. Now, with this small amount—less than a drop—of drier on the knife, tap the knifepoint next to each patty of paint. The spot of drier should be the size of a freckle, no more. If your palette is waxed, the drier will bleed out a bit; it won't on a matte surface. Use only this tiny amount and NO MORE. You want the palette to stay workable for many hours and yet, with the sparse amounts of paint we apply, have the painting dry overnight.

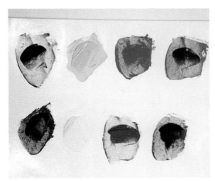

3. Now work the drier into the paint thoroughly, right away, before it dries on the palette. Notice how, after mixing it in, I scrape the paint up into a tight pile. That leaves less surface area exposed to drying and extends the life of the palette even further. Wipe the palette knife thoroughly between colors. Now you are ready to paint.

How to Keep Your Palette Fresh

If you must stop painting for a while, cover the palette to reduce exposure to air. Since cobalt drier is an oxidizer (drying the paint on contact with the air) the more airtight you can keep the palette, the longer you can extend the life of the paint. A palette keeper with a tight fitting lid for the 9 x 12-inch (22.9cm x 30.5cm) palette is something in which you may want to invest.

The paint will dry quicker on exposure to heat. Keeping the palette cool will preserve it. Conversely, if you want your painting to dry quicker, put it in a warm place.

If you cannot finish your painting within a day or two, simply toss out the old paint and put out fresh, since the drier eventually makes the palette unworkable. If you store the palette in a palette keeper, keep it cool, and do not use drier, the paint will stay workable almost indefinitely. If a color becomes sticky, use the palette knife to mix in a drop of thinner; it will reconstitute it for another painting session.

A painting surface has a certain amount of tooth and will hold only so much paint stuck down to that surface. Any excess paint you apply over and above that simply slides around, mixing too readily with other colors. It makes what oil painters refer to as "mud." Mud comes from getting too much paint on the brush and thereby transferring too much of it to the surface.

Birds are very detailed creatures. If you apply the base colors too thick, all the surface detail of feather lines and body texture will simply blend into the basecoat and disappear.

Painting realistic birds and flowers in oils means learning to paint with sparse, small amounts of paint so you have maximum control over the detail to go on top. Notice in the photos that I have little if any paint visible on the brush. I load one side only, and I load only a small amount of dry paint. Dry paint on a dry brush results in good control.

The best way to control the amount of paint you pick up is by loading your brush from loading zones.

USING A "DIRTY BRUSH"

Do not get in the habit of washing out your brights between colors or when you reload. Washing out the brush removes the dirty color, which is just what you need to help tone and control the strong intensities in your painting. If you pick up clean color at every step, you will have a much more difficult time keeping your colors compatible and controlled.

Keep the lid on the thinner and your flat brushes out of it for the most part.

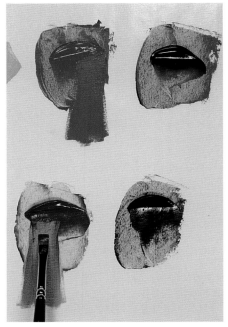

1. This is what a loading zone looks like. I've picked up just a tad of Raw Sienna and pulled it down to create a strip of sparse color, using a no. 4 bright. Work the paint until the loading zone is flat and dry and the paint evenly distributed. The purpose, remember, is to reduce the amount of paint you carry, so the loading zone should contain no excess. The best way to tell if you've got the right amount of paint is to check the surface: the main patty of paint will be shiny; the loading zone should be a dry-looking matte finish.

You should be able to pick up enough paint from a dry loading zone for eight or ten applications of paint before the area becomes too dry. Then go up to the patty and pull down just a smidgen of paint, to "feed" the loading zone. Distribute this throughout the zone and again you're ready to load your brush. Don't add more paint to the loading zone until it becomes difficult to get paint off the brush and onto the surface.

The process of creating a loading zone puts excess paint in the brush. Always dry wipe the brush on paper towels and reload in the sparse zone before going to your painting surface.

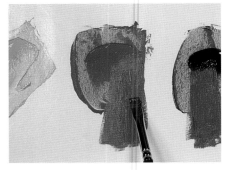

2. Here you see two loading zones, one made from the Winsor Red and one from the Alizarin Crimson. They were done as before. Squeeze the brush dry between folds of the paper towel to remove excess paint after you've made each loading zone.

3. To make a mix of the two colors, pull the brush through the Winsor Red loading zone, then the Alizarin Crimson, then back to the Winsor Red, and back to the Alizarin Crimson. Now you've created a mix of the two colors. If you desire a darker mix, load last in the Alizarin Crimson loading zone. If it's a brighter red you need, load last in the Winsor Red. The color you load last will be the majority color on the brush.

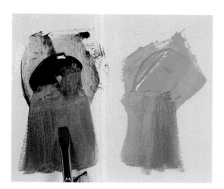

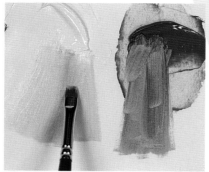

4. Sometimes it's easier to take some paint to another part of the palette to facilitate mixing. Here I've picked up a little glob of Raw Sienna on my brush, and carried it to the Sap Green. Now I'm making a "double" loading zone, pulling a little of each color down and working between them until I have a fairly even mix of the two. When you need to load repeatedly in a same or similar mix, this is often an efficient way of doing it. Plus you can make instant intensity adjustments by adding a bit more of one hue or the other.

5. The dry-wiped brush you see here was brought down to the white, after working in the green loading zone in the previous picture. Now I'm using it to make "Dirty Brush + White." That is a term you will see often in the instructions and it just means that you'll have a little of whatever color or mix you've been using left on the brush—and you'll use that to tint the white for highlighting.

Since white is very strong, you may need to remove some of it from your brush before reloading in dark mixes, or moving to a translucent color such as Raw Sienna.

Brush Care

When you've finished painting for the day, rinse the dirty brushes first in the thinner you used while painting. Then empty the tiny vial onto a paper towel and wipe it out. Refill with clean thinner and rinse your brushes once more. (Save that thinner for the next painting session.)

Then you'll need to clean your brush in an oily cleaner, since odorless thinner does not clean ALL the paint out of the brush. An oily cleaner floats the remaining paint from deep in the ferrule. I like Turpenoid Natural, a non-toxic liquid that can be used both for cleaning and for an oil medium.

Artgel is another product that cleans brushes very well, but is truly a wonder for taking the oil paint out of my clothing and off my hands.

THINNING THE PAINT

Here's what to do when the instructions say a color or mix should be "slightly thinned": Dip a clean round brush into the odorless thinner. Take the wet brush to the edge of the desired color on the palette and mix the thinner into it to make a puddle of thinned paint. Wipe the round brush on the paper towel. Now go back and roll just the tip of the brush into the slightly-thinned paint and use it for the detail.

6. Here I've made a loading zone that extends from the Black, and worked a little Raw Umber into it, a commonly used basecoat. Then, for highlighting, I simply wipe the brush dry, go into the other side of the white zone, and you have another hue of "Dirty Brush + White."

Bird Painting Basics

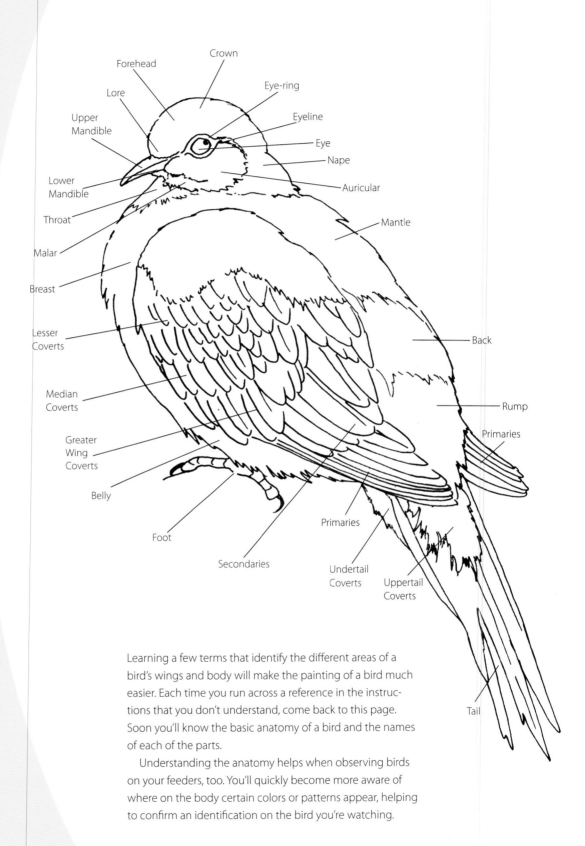

Forehead
Crown
Lore
Eye-ring
Eyeline
Upper Mandible
Eye
Nape
Lower Mandible
Auricular
Throat
Mantle
Malar
Breast
Back
Lesser Coverts
Median Coverts
Rump
Greater Wing Coverts
Primaries
Belly
Foot
Primaries
Secondaries
Undertail Coverts
Uppertail Coverts
Tail

Learning a few terms that identify the different areas of a bird's wings and body will make the painting of a bird much easier. Each time you run across a reference in the instructions that you don't understand, come back to this page. Soon you'll know the basic anatomy of a bird and the names of each of the parts.

Understanding the anatomy helps when observing birds on your feeders, too. You'll quickly become more aware of where on the body certain colors or patterns appear, helping to confirm an identification on the bird you're watching.

Feather Growth Direction

Birds' feathers grow in certain directions depending on where they are on the body. Study the original carefully; your painting will look more realistic if all your brush strokes follow the natural lie of the feathers.

I paint all bird feathers with the chisel edge of the brush held parallel to the direction shown by the arrows in this diagram. The painting is the American Robin, demonstrated step-by-step on pages 96-103.

The auricular feathers sweep back to cover the bird's ear, protecting it, and transmitting sound to it.

Ear

Lateral growth direction: a 30- to 35-degree angle.

These areas are too narrow to indicate true growth direction. Use the brush's chisel edge to detail feather lines only for most primaries.

The soft body feathers of a bird have a particular growth direction on the head, throat, breast and back. Keeping the correct growth direction is very important; you'll find it referred to in every lesson.

Creating Wing and Tail Feathers

Wing and tail feathers are stiffer, harder flight feathers that have the strength to propel the bird's weight and to control in-flight direction changes. As a result, we paint them differently than the softer body feathers. And please, use your best brush with a perfect chisel. An old scruffy brush won't work, ever, no matter how hard you try.

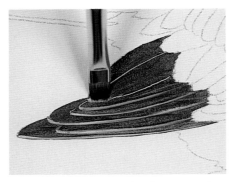

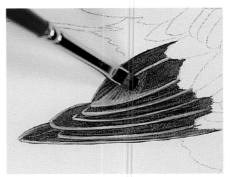

1. Basecoat: Base the primaries with a sparse but uniform basecoat of paint, drawing in the feather lines, as you cover them, using a stylus.

2. Feather edge lines: Feather lines are nothing more than a line made with sparse paint by the chisel edge of the bright. The more perfect the chisel on your brush, the better. And the less paint you load, the better. Load at a low angle to the palette in a very sparse loading zone. Then, holding the brush at a 45-degree angle (see the diagram below), begin the line at the tip of each feather and drag the brush steadily toward the base, lifting gradually as you reach the end of the line. Made a messy one? Don't worry. Just retouch with the dark base mix when you've done them all.

3. Lateral feather texture: If the feather has a visible lateral growth direction, pull those feather lines with a smaller brush so the chisel edge fits easily within the width of the feather. Make lines very close together to create the appearance of the feather fiber. For these feathers, I allow the feather edge line, which is done first, to be slightly wider than for the narrow primaries. Then I "borrow" about half of that line of paint to pull the lateral feather texture, which is partly paint and partly just marks made in the surface of the paint by the brush.

Right! A 45-degree angle to the surface produces a perfect feather line.

Load the flat side of the brush in a very dry loading zone.

Wrong! Never hold the chisel vertically for feather lines.

Never use a liner brush. The sable brights softly blend the feather lines and make them more realistic.

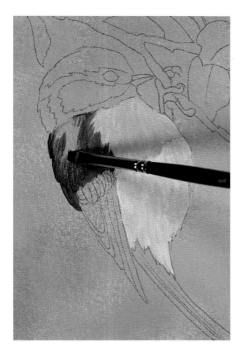

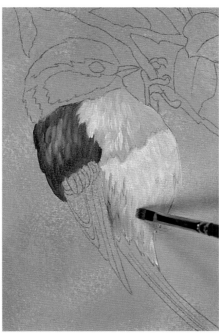

1. Body areas on a bird are fluffy and soft, much different looking than the hard flight feathers. To duplicate that look, I apply the basecoat with the chisel, using short strokes and chopping a bit at the surface as I apply the paint, all the while holding the chisel of the brush parallel to the lie of the feathers in that area.

2. Now add the Light Ivory in a different place. When blending between values, I wipe the brush dry, then use the same choppy brush stroke to blend on the line where values meet, again following growth direction, and using a brushstroke length that roughly corresponds to the length of the feathers in each area.

3. Here I've placed the final white highlight and am blending the edges of it in the same manner as before. Blend with a dry-wiped brush. Chop that chisel! Make brush tracks to indicate feather growth and texture, and don't feel compelled to blend the surface smooth. In class we say, "think fluff."

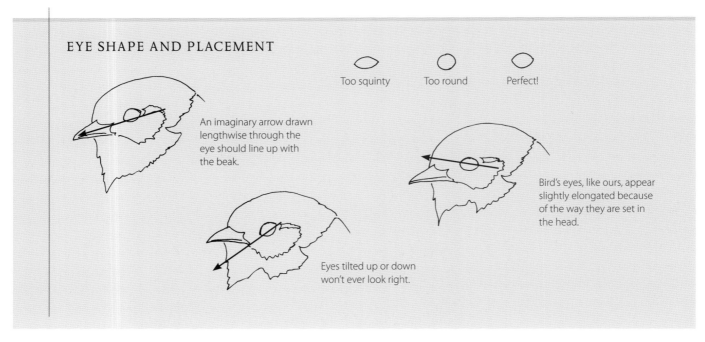

EYE SHAPE AND PLACEMENT

Too squinty   Too round   Perfect!

An imaginary arrow drawn lengthwise through the eye should line up with the beak.

Eyes tilted up or down won't ever look right.

Bird's eyes, like ours, appear slightly elongated because of the way they are set in the head.

12 Steps to Painting Birds

Each section of a bird's feathers overlap the ones below. . . so you should start painting at the tail of the bird and work toward the head to get the proper overlaps and the most realistic look to your bird.

Here's the sequence in which I paint my songbirds. If you follow this order when you paint any bird, you will never go wrong.

1. Begin by basing the tail, and detail those feather lines.

2. Base the primaries and finalize their feather edge lines.

3. Next, do the covert feathers, working one row at a time, starting with the bottom row.

4. Overlay the scapulars on top of the coverts.

5. Paint the legs and feet.

6. Base the belly and finalize the shading and highlights.

7. Base the breast, shade and highlight, then connect it to the belly feathers. (If the bird's rump and back show in the design you're painting, do those next.)

8. Now comes the all-important eye and beak. Doing them first gives you room to work.

9. Paint the rest of the head.

10. Let's give the bird a perch.

11. Then the floral elements.

12. And finally the leaves. You can do it. It's like eating an elephant: One bite at a time!

Sherry C. Nelson

Red-Breasted Nuthatch

BACKGROUND PREPARATION

Surface:
9" x 12" (23cm × 30cm)
hardboard panel,
⅛" (3mm) thick

Delta Ceramcoat
acrylic paints:
Moss Green
Gamal Green
Seminole Green
Flesh Tan

FOR PROJECT

Winsor & Newton
Artists' Oils:
Ivory Black
Titanium White
Raw Sienna
Raw Umber
Burnt Sienna
Sap Green
Cadmium Yellow Pale
French Ultramarine

Brushes:
nos. 2, 4, 6, 8 red sable
  brights
no. 0 red sable round

CLOSE COUSIN TO THE CHICKADEES, the nuthatches are engaging, acrobatic birds of both forest and garden. Their odd name comes from the habit of placing a nut or seed in a bark crevice and using the sharp beak to hack it open. Unlike woodpeckers and creepers who work their way up trees, the nuthatches feed upside down, effortlessly working their way down the underside of a branch. They are even known to roost head downward.

Black + Raw Umber + French Ultramarine

Dirty brush (previous mix) + White

Black + French Ultramarine + White

Burnt Sienna + Raw Sienna

Raw Sienna + Cadmium Yellow Pale + White

Raw Umber + White

Black + Raw Umber

Black + Sap Green

Sap Green + Raw Sienna + White

Dark green mix (previous mix) + more White

French Ultramarine + White

Raw Sienna + White

Raw Sienna + Cadmium Yellow Pale

Line Drawing

This line drawing may be hand-traced or photocopied for personal use only. It is shown here at full size. Transfer to your prepared background using dark graphite paper. Be especially careful when transferring all the detail of the eye, beak and head. The more accurate the transfer, the better the painting.

Field Sketches

BROWN CREEPER
The Brown Creeper earns his name—energetically creeping up and around tree branches, probing into bark crevices for his favorite insects and spiders. A distant cousin to the nuthatches.

Many small moths are beautifully patterned. They make exciting elements to add to any bird painting.

PYGMY NUTHATCH
A tiny little guy, he lives with his family group in a nuthatch "apartment house" in the pines.

WHITE-BREASTED NUTHATCH
Common at feeders everywhere—loves those sunflower seeds!

Tail, Wing and Breast

PREPARE THE BACKGROUND

Base the hardboard panel with Moss Green, using a sponge roller. Let dry, sand well. Rebase, and while wet, drizzle on a 1-inch (25mm) stripe of Seminole Green at the edge of the surface in two places. Blend green into basecoat with same roller.

Next add a little Gamal Green within the previous green areas, again blending to achieve nice value gradations between the added greens and the background. Finally drizzle a little Flesh Tan in the central area of the surface and blend it here and there into the background. Let dry, sand well, and spray with Liberty Matte Finish.

1 **Tail:** Using a no. 4 bright, base dark value with Black + Raw Umber + French Ultramarine. Base light value on underside of tail using the dirty brush + more White. Base undertail coverts with White.

Wing: With a no. 4 bright, base with Black + French Ultramarine + White. Mark in feather lines with stylus as you cover them with paint.

Breast: Base with Burnt Sienna + Raw Sienna, using a no. 4 bright.

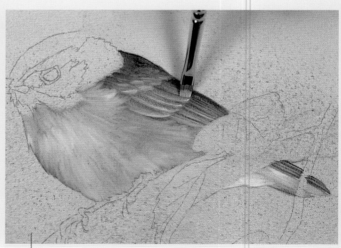

2 **Tail:** Streak in feather lines on tail with dirty brush + White.

Wing: Shade along outer edge of wing with Black + French Ultramarine.

Breast: Highlight with Raw Sienna + Cadmium Yellow Pale + White.

3 **Wing:** Lay in feather lines using the chisel edge of a no. 4 and small amounts of dirty White. Use the same mix on the corner of the brush to chop in smaller covert marks.

Breast: Blend the highlights with short strokes, following the growth direction of the feathers. Fluff some breast feathering over edge of wing to soften. Shade with a little Raw Umber along the outer edges of the breast (see the finished painting on page 24).

Head and Feet

Black + Raw Umber

Black + Raw Umber + French Ultramarine

Eye-ring: White + Raw Umber

Black + Raw Umber

Highlight with White

Shade with Black + Raw Umber

White

Highlight with White

1. Paint the eye-ring first, using the round brush for the eye detail. Use a no. 2 bright to paint the other head areas.

2. Base eye with Black. Base remaining areas as shown. Blend the shading on crown and forehead to create a value gradation.

3. Highlight eye with White dot using round brush. Highlight on crown and cheek with White, and blend to create soft, fluffy value gradations.

1. Base with Raw Umber, using a no. 2 bright.

2. Highlight with dirty brush + White.

3. Add detail lines and toenails with Raw Umber, slightly thinned, using the round brush. Highlight toenails with a bit of dirty White.

Noctuid Moth, Foliage and Flower Bud

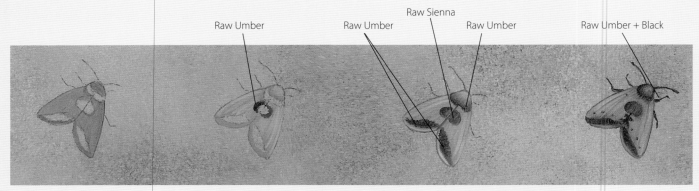

Raw Umber

Raw Umber   Raw Sienna   Raw Umber

Raw Umber + Black

1. Base the Noctuid Moth with Raw Sienna + Cadmium Yellow Pale using the no. 2 bright.

2. Highlight wings and head using dirty brush + White. Streak highlights on wings using chisel edge. Detail wings with Raw Umber spot, using round brush.

3. Add additional details with Raw Umber and Raw Sienna.

4. Detail the tiny spots and fine lines on the wings with Raw Umber, using the round brush. Add legs and antennae with Raw Umber + Black.

1

Branch: Base with slightly-thinned Raw Umber, using the no. 6 bright.

Leaves: Using a no. 4, base the dark value with Black + Sap Green. Base the light value with Sap Green + Raw Sienna + White or a mix of French Ultramarine + White.

Stems: Base with Black + Sap Green, using the no. 4 bright.

Bud: Base dark value with Black + Sap Green, using the no. 2 bright. Base the light value with Sap Green + Raw Sienna + White. Base the calyx with Raw Sienna.

Foliage and Final Blending

2 **Branch:** Detail branch by chopping bark-like marks of unthinned Raw Umber, and Raw Umber + White.

Leaves: Blend between values, with the growth direction, using the chisel edge of the brush. Lay in highlight areas using Sap Green + White or French Ultramarine + White.

Stems: Highlight down center of each stem with Sap Green + Raw Sienna + White.

Bud: Blend between values, then highlight with light green mix. Highlight the calyx with Raw Sienna + White.

3 **Branch:** Do final blending to create realistic texture.

Leaves: Blend the highlights. Add central vein structure with chisel edge, using the light value green mix. Accent with a little Burnt Sienna if desired.

Stems and Bud: Do any final blending needed.

Finish: Before painting is dry, clean up any graphite lines or messy edges with the no. 8 bright, dipped in odorless thinner and blotted on a paper towel.

Sherry C. Nelson

Blue Tit

BACKGROUND PREPARATION

Surface:
9" x 12" (23cm x 30cm) hardboard panel, ⅛" (3mm) thick

Delta Ceramcoat acrylic paints:
Moss Green
Tide Pool Blue
Light Ivory

FOR PROJECT

Winsor & Newton Artists' Oils:
Ivory Black
Titanium White
Raw Sienna
Raw Umber
Sap Green
Cadmium Yellow Pale
Winsor Red
French Ultramarine

Brushes:
nos. 2, 4, 6, 8 red sable brights
no. 0 red sable round

A WIDESPREAD EUROPEAN CHICKADEE, the beautiful Blue Tit is one of the most common and best-loved garden birds in England. They are noted for their confident, fearless nature, and willingly use nest boxes and come to feeders. Highly intelligent, the Blue Tits have been used in scientific studies, demonstrating that they can complete a precise and complex sequence of more than 25 tasks to get the reward—a sunflower seed—at the end!

Raw Umber + French Ultramarine + Titanium White

French Ultramarine + White

Dirty brush (from previous mix) + White

Raw Umber + Ivory Black

Raw Umber + Sap Green

Cadmium Yellow Pale + White

Raw Umber + White

Black + Sap Green

Sap Green + Raw Sienna

Raw Sienna + White

Dirty brush + French Ultramarine + White

Black + Raw Umber

Dirty brush + White

Sap Green + White

Winsor Red + Raw Umber

This line drawing may be hand-traced or photocopied for personal use only. Enlarge at 111% to bring it up to full size. Transfer to your prepared background using dark graphite paper. Be especially careful when transferring all the detail of the eye, beak and head. The more accurate the transfer, the better the painting.

Field Sketches

This Black-capped Chickadee is a North American cousin of the Blue Tit. At a glance, you can see the similarity in body shape and sense the bold, active behavior that characterizes the whole family.

GREAT TIT
I've spotted the Great Tit in England as well as in Japan, which tells the story of its wide distribution across all of Eurasia, into India and Indonesia. The dramatic central black breast stripe makes for an easy identification no matter what country you see it in.

COAL TIT
The little Coal Tit is the smallest of the family. It nests in cavities like most all the tits, and though shy, appreciates a good feeder spread. Favorite foods include caterpillars, beetles and other insects.

Tail and Wing

PREPARE THE BACKGROUND

Base the hardboard panel with Moss Green, using a sponge roller. Let dry. Sand well. Rebase, and while wet, drizzle on a 2-inch (51mm) stripe of Tide Pool Blue in two different places on the surface. Use the same roller to blend blue softly here and there into the basecoat. Now add a little Light Ivory in the center of the surface, again blending and moving color around to achieve nice value gradations between the splotches of Light Ivory and the background. Let dry, sand well, and spray with Liberty Matte Finish.

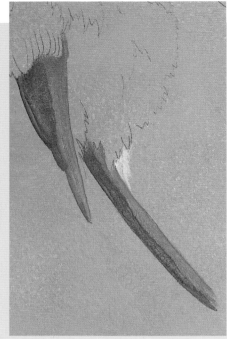

1 **Tail:** Using a no. 4 bright, base dark value with Raw Umber + French Ultramarine + little White. Base light value on underside of tail with the dark mix + more White. Base undertail coverts with White.

Wing: Base with same mixes used for tail, using the same brush. Mark in feather lines with stylus as you cover them with paint.

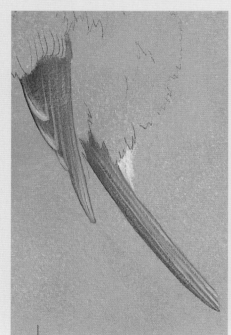

2 **Tail:** Streak in feather lines on tail with dirty brush + White. Shade topside of tail with Black + Raw Umber.

Wing: Streak in feather lines with dirty brush + White. Widen secondary lines with more White. Shade along outer edge of wing with Black + Raw Umber.

3 **Tail:** Shade with additional Black + Raw Umber on topside of tail.

Wing: Shade with additional Black + Raw Umber on secondaries. Base the dark value of the coverts with Raw Umber + French Ultramarine + a little White. Base the light value with the same mix + additional French Ultramarine + White.

Belly, Breast and Back

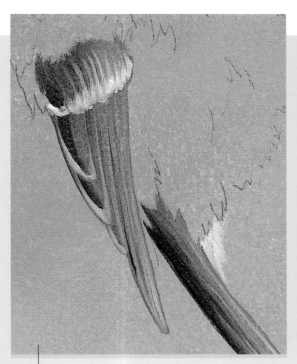

1   Using a no. 2 bright, base the wingbar with White, then pull white lines upward using the wingbar paint to define the covert feather lines.

2   **Belly:** Using the no. 4 bright, base with White.
Breasts: Base with White + Cadmium Yellow Pale, using the no. 4 bright.
Back: With the same brush, base the back with Raw Umber + Sap Green.

3   **Belly:** Shade the belly with choppy strokes of Raw Umber + White on the no. 4 bright, following the growth direction of the feathering and creating texture that will build form and shape.
Breast: Highlight the breast with pure White, again chopping with the chisel edge of the brush, and creating texture and growth direction.
Back: Highlight the back of the bird with Cadmium Yellow Pale + White, working to create form and shape with choppy strokes of the corner of the brush.

Head, Feet and Ladybug

Black + Raw Umber

Eye-ring: White + Raw Umber

Black + Raw Umber

White

Highlight with White

Raw Umber + Sap Green

French Ultramarine + Raw Umber

1. Base the eye-ring first with White + Raw Umber on a no. 0 round. Base eye with Black. Base the dark markings on head and beak with Black + Raw Umber on no. 2 bright. As you base in front and behind eye, use the dark mix to narrow the width of the eye-ring so just a hairline is left at top and bottom and a bit wider front and back.

2. Base areas above eye and on cheek and upper mandible of beak with White. Use the chisel edge of the no. 2 to connect the White and Black areas in tiny irregular zig-zags. Do not allow colors to blend together.

3. Base the crown with French Ultramarine + Raw Umber on a no. 2. Highlight with White. Base the nape with Raw Umber + Sap Green. Highlight nape with Raw Sienna + White. Blend between dark and light values on beak. Re-highlight beak with White if needed.

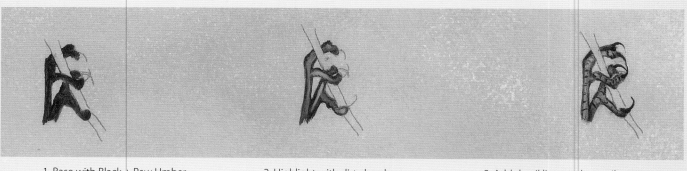

1. Base with Black + Raw Umber on a no. 2 bright.

2. Highlight with dirty brush + White.

3. Add detail lines and toenails with Black + Raw Umber, slightly thinned, on a round brush.

1. Outline with Winsor Red + Raw Umber, using the no. 0 bright. Fill in with Winsor Red.

2. Blend where values meet.

3. With no. 0 round, highlight with White down the center line of the back and along the edges of wings. Base head with Black.

4. Detail tiny spots, antennae and legs with Black, and highlight back with White.

Leaves, Flowers and Final Blending

1 **Branch:** With a no. 6, base dark value with Raw Umber. Chop in light value with Raw Sienna + White.

Leaves: With a no. 4, base the dark value with Black + Sap Green. Base the light value with Sap Green + Raw Sienna + White or a mix of French Ultramarine + White.

Stems: Base with Black + Sap Green, using a no. 2 bright.

Blossoms: Base dark value with Sap Green + Raw Sienna on no. 2. Base light value of some with Cadmium Yellow Pale + White, and others with pure Cadmium Yellow Pale.

2 **Branch:** Chop values together with chisel edge of brush to create realistic texture.

Leaves: Blend between values, with the growth direction, using the chisel edge of the brush.

Blossoms: Blend between values to create gradation within each petal.

3 **Branch:** Highlight with choppy textured dirty White.

Leaves: Add highlights with a pale mix of White + French Ultramarine.

Stems: Highlight down center of each stem with Sap Green + Raw Sienna + White.

Blossoms: Highlight with White or a pale mix of White + Cadmium Yellow Pale.

4 **Branch:** Do any final blending needed to create realistic texture.

Leaves: Blend highlights with growth direction and add central vein with light leaf mix.

Blossoms: Blend highlights to create final gradations in each petal.

Finish: Before painting is dry, clean up any graphite lines or messy edges with a no. 8 bright dipped in odorless thinner and blotted on a paper towel.

European Robin

BACKGROUND PREPARATION

Surface:
9" x 12" (23cm x 30cm)
hardboard panel, 1/8"
(3mm) thick

Delta Ceramcoat acrylic paints:
Trail Tan
Light Ivory

FOR PROJECT

Winsor & Newton Artists' Oils:
Ivory Black
Titanium White
Raw Sienna
Raw Umber
Burnt Sienna
Sap Green
Cadmium Yellow Pale
Winsor Red
French Ultramarine

Brushes:
nos. 0, 2, 4, 6, 8 red sable
   brights
no. 0 red sable round

RANGING THROUGHOUT EUROPE and familiar even to non-birders, the beautiful Robin is the national bird of Britain. Tame and bold, this vocal mite willingly dogs the footsteps of a gardener in hopes of the spade turning over a bit of lunch. The first colonists named the American Robin after this familiar dooryard bird of Europe. However, the two species are not closely related, and our Robins are in fact much larger. I remember with great pleasure my first sighting of this lovely songster in the spring gardens of Kew, proclaiming his ownership of a nesting territory. Perfect for a book on songbirds!

Raw Umber + Sap Green

Raw Sienna + White

Raw Umber + White

Burnt Sienna + Raw Umber

Black + White

Cadmium Yellow Pale + Winsor Red + Raw Sienna

Winsor Red + Burnt Sienna

Cadmium Yellow Pale + White

Black + Raw Umber

Black + Raw Umber + White

Black + Sap Green

Sap Green + Raw Sienna + White

Sap Green + Raw Sienna + more White

White + Black + tad of French Ultramarine

This line drawing may be hand-traced or photocopied for personal use only. Enlarge at 105% to bring it up to full size. Transfer to your prepared background using dark graphite paper. Be especially careful when transferring all the detail of the eye, beak and head. The more accurate the transfer, the better the painting.

Field Sketches

Apple Blossoms photo by Deborah A. Galloway

Shoot a lot of reference photos like this one when the fruit trees bloom in the spring. Useful with many kinds of bird paintings, you can't have too many flower photos!

THE BLUETHROAT

A fairly common bird in many parts of Europe, the striking throat pattern is a distinctive, reliable field mark. Deb Galloway and I saw this bird as a rare migrant on the remote island of St. Lawrence off the coast of Alaska. Unforgettable!

COMMON NIGHTINGALE

The Nightingale's song, considered one of the finest in the avian world, is heard far more often than the bird is seen, since it prefers to remain hidden in dense bushes and brush in parks and woodland. The young Nightingale closely resembles a juvenile Robin.

NORTHERN WHEATEAR

Wheatears are small, ground-dwelling birds found in open country. These guys are very active, frequently bowing and flicking the tail. I sketched this one at Minsmere, a fabulous bird reserve on the North Sea in Britain.

Tail, Wings and Belly

PREPARE THE BACKGROUND

Base the hardboard panel, using a sponge roller, with Trail Tan. Let dry, sand well. Rebase, and while wet, drizzle on a 2-inch (51mm) stripe of Light Ivory on the surface in two different places. Blend into the basecoat with the same roller, moving color here and there to distribute the highlight. Let dry, sand well, and spray with Liberty Matte Finish. Refer to the chapter on Preparing the Background for additional information on surface preparation.

1

Tail: Using a no. 4 bright, base with Raw Umber + Sap Green.

Primaries: Base with Raw Umber + Sap Green, using a no. 4. Mark in feather lines with stylus as you cover them with paint.

Coverts: Base dark value with Raw Umber + Sap Green, using the no. 2. Use stylus to mark in feather lines. Base light value with Raw Sienna + White.

Scapulars: Base with Raw Umber + Sap Green, using the no. 2.

Undertail Coverts: Base with White, using the no. 2.

Belly: Base dark value with Raw Umber + Sap Green. Base light value with White, using the no. 4.

2

Tail: Streak in feather lines on the tail with Raw Umber + White using the chisel edge of the brush.

Primaries: Streak in feather lines with Raw Umber + White.

Coverts: Blend a bit between values using chisel edge. Then streak in feather lines with White + Raw Umber using the chisel edge.

Scapulars: Shade with Raw Umber + Burnt Sienna. Accent across the scapulars in two bands: Raw Sienna toward bottom and Burnt Sienna higher up. Then chop on a faint row of marks with dirty White to indicate smaller feathers at bottom of area. Add a second row, more faint, above that.

Undertail Coverts: Blend a little at base to connect to belly feathers. Highlight with White.

Belly: Blend with choppy strokes of the chisel where values meet, gradually creating a value gradation. Shade next to wing with Raw Umber. Highlight with White.

Belly, Breast and Flank

1 **Belly:** Blend the shading with choppy strokes where it meets the basecoat, creating a value gradation. Blend the highlights with short strokes, following the growth direction of the feathers. Fluff some breast feathering over the edge of the wing to soften. Think texture!

Breast: Base with Cadmium Yellow Pale + Winsor Red + Raw Sienna. Shade with Winsor Red + Burnt Sienna. Highlight with Cadmium Yellow Pale + White.

Gray Flank: Base with Black + White.

2 **Breast:** Blend where values meet between highlight and basecoat and shading and basecoat. Use choppy short strokes of the chisel and follow growth direction of the feathers and create form and shape. Shade with Burnt Sienna if needed to control intensity of orange.

Gray Flank: Highlight this with a bit of White, and with same short strokes, blend to connect this area to the orange breast. Fluff some gray feathering over the edge of the wing.

Head and Feet

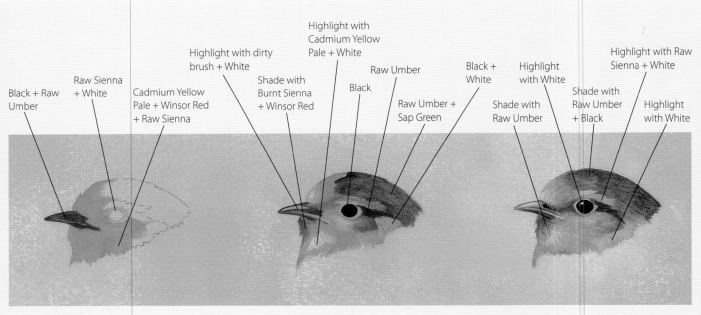

Black + Raw Umber

Raw Sienna + White

Cadmium Yellow Pale + Winsor Red + Raw Sienna

Highlight with dirty brush + White

Shade with Burnt Sienna + Winsor Red

Highlight with Cadmium Yellow Pale + White

Black

Raw Umber

Raw Umber + Sap Green

Black + White

Highlight with White

Shade with Raw Umber

Highlight with Raw Sienna + White

Shade with Raw Umber + Black

Highlight with White

1. Paint the eye-ring first, using the round brush for the eye detail. Use the no. 2 bright to paint the other head areas.

2. Base eye with Black. Base remaining areas as shown.

3. Highlight eye with White dot using round brush. Blend the beak where values meet. Rehighlight beak with White if needed. Blend orange values on face with growth direction. Shade under beak with Raw Umber. Highlight gray area with dirty brush + White and blend. Shade the crown with Raw Umber + Black. Highlight with Raw Sienna + White. Blend between values to create a value gradation.

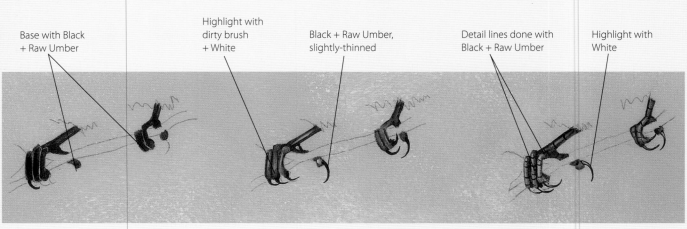

Base with Black + Raw Umber

Highlight with dirty brush + White

Black + Raw Umber, slightly-thinned

Detail lines done with Black + Raw Umber

Highlight with White

1. Base with Black + Raw Umber on a no. 2 bright.

2. Highlight with dirty brush + White. Do toenails with slightly-thinned dark mix, using the round brush.

3. Add detail lines on legs with dark mix, slightly thinned, using the round brush. Highlight toenails with a bit of dirty White.

Apple Blossoms and Foliage

1

Branch: Base dark value with Raw Umber and light value with Burnt Sienna, using the no. 4.

Leaves: Using a no. 4, base the dark value with Black + Sap Green. Base some light value areas with Sap Green + Raw Sienna + White. Base others with a mix of Black + White + a bit of French Ultramarine.

Stems and Calyxes: Base with same mixes used for leaves, using the no. 2.

Blossoms: Using the no. 4 or no. 2 for smaller petals, base the darker shadow areas at base of petals and under overlapping petals with Black + White. Base rest of each petal with White.

2

Branch: Detail branch with chopping bark-like marks of the dry brush. Highlight with Raw Sienna + White.

Leaves: Blend between values, with the growth direction, using the chisel edge of the brush. Lay in highlight areas using the light value blue mix + more White.

Stems: Highlight down center of each stem with same light value blue mix used for leaves.

Blossoms: Blend between values, then highlight with White.

3

Branch: Do final blending to create realistic texture.

Leaves: Blend the highlights. Add central vein structure with chisel edge, using the light value green mix.

Stems: Do any final blending needed.

Blossoms: Blend the highlights where values meet. Shade in some shadow areas with a little Raw Sienna to warm blossoms.

Finish: Before painting is dry, clean up any graphite lines or messy edges with the no. 8 bright dipped in odorless thinner and blotted on a paper towel.

Sherry C. Nelson

Blue Jay

BACKGROUND PREPARATION

Surface:
9" x 12" (23cm x 30cm) hardboard panel, ⅛" (3mm) thick

Delta Ceramcoat acrylic paints:
Moss Green
Williamsburg Blue
Light Ivory

FOR PROJECT

Winsor & Newton Artists' Oils:
Ivory Black
Titanium White
Raw Sienna
Raw Umber
Burnt Sienna
Sap Green
French Ultramarine

Brushes:
nos. 2, 4, 6, 8 red sable brights
no. 1 red sable round

THE RASCALLY BLUE JAY INCITES ALL SORTS OF reactions from the folks who host them at their feeders and observe them on a daily basis. One thing is for sure, they are beautiful, with a spectacular cerulean blue plumage that's positively iridescent against a winter landscape. Fascinating, really, that all blue in all birds is a result of the action of light on the individual cells of the plumage; each feather cell breaks up the light into the spectrum and reflects back only the blue light to the observer's eye. There is no such thing as blue pigmented feathering in the world of birds.

Raw Umber + Raw Sienna

Black + Raw Umber

Dirty brush + White

Raw Umber + French Ultramarine

Dirty brush + White

Black + Sap Green

Burnt Sienna + Raw Umber

Sap Green + Raw Sienna + White

Green Mix + more White

Raw Sienna + White

Raw Umber + White

Raw Umber + French Ultramarine + White

Raw Umber + French Ultramarine + more White

Line Drawing

This line drawing may be hand-traced or photocopied for personal use only. Enlarge at 111% to bring it up to full size. Transfer to your prepared background using dark graphite paper. Be especially careful when transferring all the detail of the eye, beak and head. The more accurate the transfer, the better the painting.

Field Sketches

STELLAR'S JAY
Another species found in mountainous western North America, this beautiful dark bird is our only jay with an entirely black head.

A typical backyard shot. . .look at that plumage glow in the subdued light! Structural color at work.

MEXICAN JAY
A quick sketch of my common yard bird here in Arizona. This lovely gray-blue jay used to be called Gray-breasted, for obvious reasons. They have an unusual social behavior. Only one or two pairs in the extended family mate and lay eggs. The others become helpers at the nest to ensure that more young survive.

GRAY JAY
A bird of the colder regions, the Rocky Mountains and most of Canada host this unusual jay. For many years it was called Canada Jay. This was the first bird species I ever painted. I have a soft spot in my heart for the one we photographed in Rocky Mountain National Park way back in 1975.

Tail, Breast, Belly and Legs

PREPARE THE BACKGROUND

Base the hardboard panel, using a sponge roller, with Moss Green. Let dry, sand well. Rebase, and while wet, drizzle on a 2-inch (51mm) stripe of Williamsburg Blue in the center of the surface. Blend into the basecoat with the same roller, moving color here and there to distribute the color and soften into the background. Then, in two places at the edge of the surface, drizzle 1 inch (25mm) of Light Ivory. Blend here and there to distribute the highlight. Let dry, sand well, and spray with Liberty Matte Finish. Refer to the chapter on Preparing the Background for additional information on surface preparation.

1 **Tail:** Using a no. 4 bright, base dark value with Raw Umber + a little Raw Sienna. Base light value with White.

Breast and Belly: Base dark value with Raw Umber + a little Raw Sienna. Base light value with White, using the no. 4.

Legs: Base with Black + Raw Umber, using the no. 2 bright.

2 **Tail:** Blend lengthwise with tail, where values meet.

Breast and Belly: Blend with choppy strokes of the brush's chisel edge where values meet, gradually creating a value gradation. Make strokes short, and carefully follow growth direction of feathers to create some shape and form even at this early stage.

Legs: Highlight with dirty brush + White.

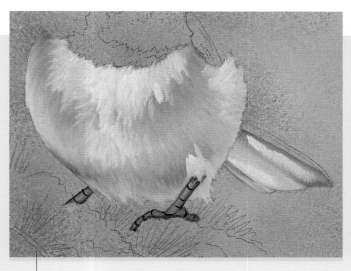

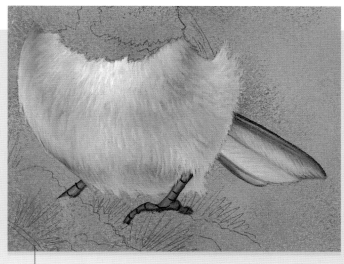

3 **Tail:** Highlight with White.
Breast and Belly: Highlight with White. Pressure paint on following growth direction of the feathers. Set the stage for what's to come.
Legs: Add detail lines on legs with dark mix, slightly thinned, using the round brush.

4 **Tail:** Blend with growth direction, using very close together lines of the chisel edge. Note how the lateral growth of the tail feather changes from side to side. Base the narrow blue edge of the tail with French Ultramarine + Raw Umber. Streak in feather lines on blue tail edge with Raw Umber + White using chisel edge of brush.
Breast and Belly: Blend where highlights meet the underlying values. Use choppy short strokes of the chisel edge and follow growth direction of the feathers and create form and shape. Think texture!

5 **Coverts:** Base wing with Raw Umber + French Ultramarine. Highlight a little with dirty brush + White. Then add detail markings with round brush using slightly-thinned Black.
Breast and Belly: Additional white "fluff" may be now be added using slightly-thinned White on the round brush. Make short, fine lines following the growth direction in the major light areas, and where the feathers fluff out to the side next to the wing. Any additional final highlights may be added when the piece is dry. Highlight with pure White and scruff into surface to blend.

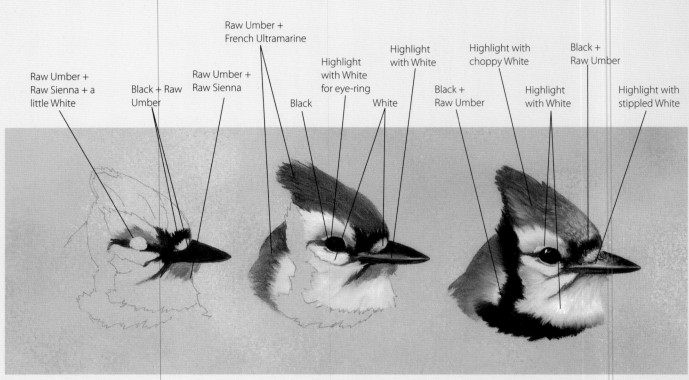

Raw Umber +
Raw Sienna + a
little White

Black + Raw
Umber

Raw Umber +
Raw Sienna

Raw Umber +
French Ultramarine

Black

Highlight
with White
for eye-ring

Highlight
with White

White

Highlight with
choppy White

Black +
Raw Umber

Black +
Raw Umber

Highlight
with White

Highlight with
stippled White

1. Using a no. 2 bright, paint above the eye, using Raw Umber + Raw Sienna + a little White. Base under the beak with Raw Umber + Raw Sienna. Base dark areas on face and beak with Black + Raw Umber.

2. Base eye with Black. Base light areas with White. Base blue areas with Raw Umber + French Ultramarine. Highlight beak with dirty White. Highlight above and below eye with a line of White.

3. Highlight eye with White dot using round brush. Blend the beak where values meet then add more highlight on upper mandible. Highlight forehead with choppy corner stroke of a no. 2 bright to indicate small feathers. Base the dark bands with Black + Raw Umber. Blend to connect colors between dark bands, white areas and blue areas. Do not overwork; just connect colors with slight movements of the chisel edge of the brush.

Blend between the blue and white on the nape of neck with growth direction of feathers.

Pine Branches and Snow

1 **Branch:** Base with Burnt Sienna + Raw Umber.
Needles: Basecoat needle areas with Black + Sap Green. Add some Raw Umber to the mix in a few areas to vary color.

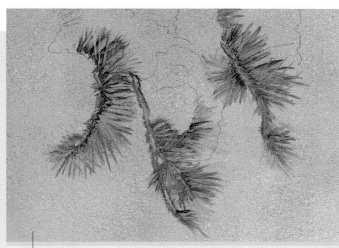

2 **Branch:** Highlight branches with Raw Sienna + White.
Needles: Use palette knife and a few drops of odorless thinner to make a thinned mix of Sap Green + Black. Make a second thinned mix of Sap Green + Raw Sienna + White. Apply first a basecoat of darker needles with the dark value, using the round brush. Extend needles slightly beyond basecoat but do not let them grow longer than the pattern. Then overlay dark needle areas with strokes of the lighter value for highlight and to vary values.

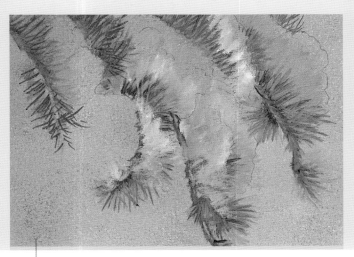

3 **Create snow with a variety of values.** Lay in darkest shadow areas with a darker value of Raw Umber + French Ultramarine + White. Once initial shadows are placed, begin to apply a lighter value of the same mix next to them.

4 **Finally, build tops of mounds of snow to pure White.** Wipe brush dry, and firmly pounce brush where values meet to blend. Try to achieve a fuzzy, granular blend, the texture of snow. Study the finished painting to see how light and how blended the snow should be. Do not overwork. It's easy to lose control of white paint, particularly when it's generously applied. Before painting is dry, clean up any graphite lines or messy edges with the no. 8 bright dipped in odorless thinner and blotted on a paper towel.

Song Sparrow

BACKGROUND PREPARATION

Surface:
9" x 12" (23cm x 30cm) hardboard panel, 1/8" (3mm) thick

Delta Ceramcoat acrylic paints:
Moss Green
Antique Rose
Light Ivory

FOR PROJECT

Winsor & Newton Artists' Oils:
Ivory Black
Titanium White
Raw Sienna
Raw Umber
Burnt Sienna
Sap Green
Cadmium Yellow Pale
Alizarin Crimson

Brushes:
nos. 2, 4, 6, 8 red sable brights
no. 0 red sable round

MOST PEOPLE THINK OF SPARROWS as being drab and uninteresting. Perhaps our negative response has to do with the often-unwelcome House Sparrow, an interloper that takes over feeders and threatens our native species. But true sparrows have fascinating patterns of feathering, lovely subtle colors and many possess beautiful and memorable songs. The little song sparrow is typical, cheerily trilling his distinctive melody from one end of North America to the other—until one is forced to take notice and finally become a convert to the sparrow's quiet beauty.

White + Raw Sienna

White + Raw Umber

Black + Raw Umber + Burnt Sienna

Burnt Sienna + Raw Umber + Raw Sienna

Previous mix + White

Black + Raw Umber

Raw Umber + a tad of Burnt Sienna

Raw Sienna + Alizarin Crimson

Previous mix + White

White + Cadmium Yellow Pale

Black + Sap Green

Sap Green + Raw Sienna + White

White + Sap Green + Raw Sienna

Alizarin Crimson + Black

Previous mix + White

This line drawing may be hand-traced or photocopied for personal use only. It is shown here full size. Transfer to your prepared background using dark graphite paper. Be especially careful when transferring all the detail of the eye, beak and head. The more accurate the transfer, the better the painting.

Field Sketches

Song Sparrow photo by Arthur Morris

WHITE-THROATED SPARROW

This was one of the first birds I saw as a beginning birder. I was entranced by the contrasting white of the throat, the striking bit of yellow at the lore. . . and not to mention, one of the finest songs of any bird. I'm a great fan of this beautiful sparrow even today, 25 years later.

Song Sparrows always seem to be singing, so it's fairly easy to catch them in such a cooperative pose. Note that the breast markings on this individual are much darker than the one in my painting. Song sparrow plumage varies widely over its extensive range, but its song does not.

BLACK-THROATED SPARROW

Smaller than some of the other sparrows, the Black-throated is a bird of the dry canyonlands and grasslands of the West—and an occasional feeder bird in my yard. He's tops on my list of paintings to come.

Tail, Wing and Rump

PREPARE THE BACKGROUND

Base the hardboard panel, using a sponge roller, with Moss Green. Let dry, sand well. Rebase, and while wet, drizzle a 2-inch (51mm) stripe of Antique Rose on the surface. Blend with the same roller to achieve good value gradations between the Rose and the background and to distribute the Rose on the surface.

Finally, drizzle a little Light Ivory in the central area of the surface and blend it here and there into the background. Let dry, sand well, and spray with Liberty Matte Finish. Refer to the chapter on Preparing the Background for additional information on surface preparation.

1 **Tail:** Using a no. 4 bright, base dark value with Raw Umber. Base rest of tail with Raw Sienna.

Undertail Coverts: Base dark value with Raw Sienna and light value with Raw Sienna + White, using the no. 4.

Primaries: Base with Raw Umber using the no. 4 bright.

Wing Coverts: Base with White, using the no. 2.

Scapulars: Base with Black + Raw Umber, using a no. 2.

Rump: Base dark value with Raw Umber and the light value with Raw Sienna, using the no. 2

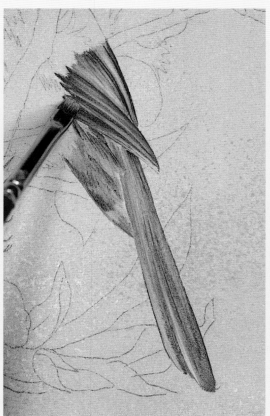

2 **Tail:** Blend between values, lengthwise with growth direction. Streak in feather lines with dirty brush + White on the chisel edge of the brush.

Undertail Coverts: Blend between values with growth, then shade with Raw Umber to indicate indistinct markings.

Primaries: Streak in feather lines with dirty brush + White on the chisel edge of the brush.

Rump: Highlight with Raw Sienna + White.

Tail, Breast and Belly

1 **Tail:** Shade the top of the tail under the wing using Raw Umber.

Undertail Coverts: Blend shading a little to break hard edges of markings into the basecoat color, following the growth direction.

Back: Lay in dark value with Raw Umber and light value with Raw Sienna, using the no. 4.

Breast and Belly: Base dark value with Raw Sienna and the light value area with Raw Sienna + White using the no. 4.

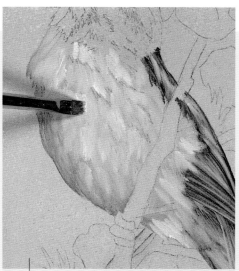

2 **Breast and Belly:** Blend where values meet, using choppy strokes and following the growth direction. Highlight with White, then blend a bit with growth direction to create form and shape.

3 **When breast highlights are complete,** center tracing paper overlay used in design transfer back on top of wet paint, being careful not to disturb paint underneath. Using a ball-point pen, retransfer the markings firmly into the wet paint.

4 **Markings:** Base carefully with slightly-thinned Raw Umber + Burnt Sienna + Black, using the no. 0 round. Do not allow dark mix to blend into the basecoat except in very tiny areas. When markings are done, use the no. 2 bright to pull a little breast color from the flank area over the narrow bands of color on the back. Reload White on the brush if more paint is needed to get a fluffy feathered look.

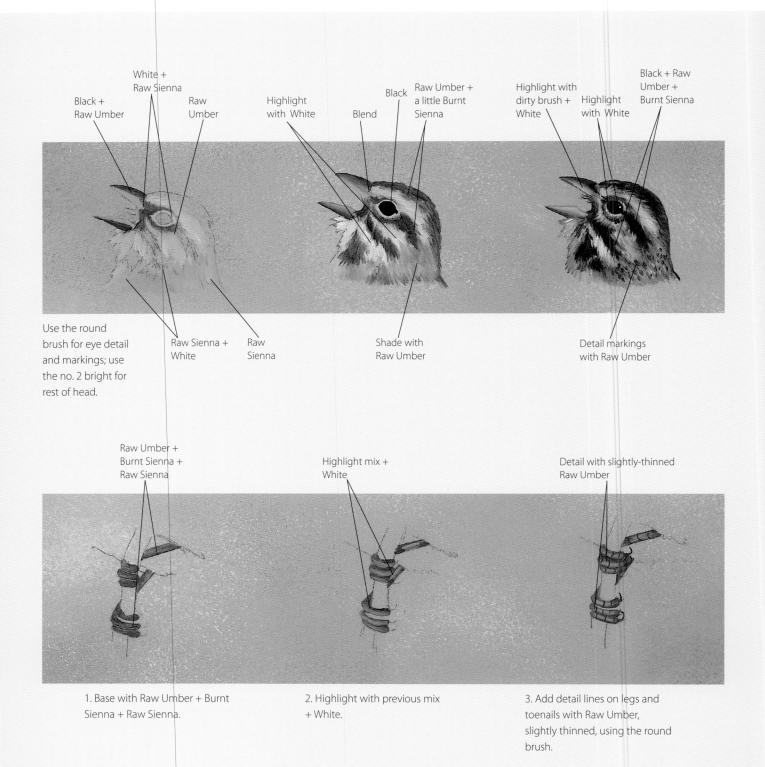

Black +
Raw Umber

White +
Raw Sienna

Raw
Umber

Highlight
with White

Blend

Black

Raw Umber +
a little Burnt
Sienna

Highlight with
dirty brush +
White

Highlight
with White

Black + Raw
Umber +
Burnt Sienna

Use the round
brush for eye detail
and markings; use
the no. 2 bright for
rest of head.

Raw Sienna +
White

Raw
Sienna

Shade with
Raw Umber

Detail markings
with Raw Umber

Raw Umber +
Burnt Sienna +
Raw Sienna

Highlight mix +
White

Detail with slightly-thinned
Raw Umber

1. Base with Raw Umber + Burnt
Sienna + Raw Sienna.

2. Highlight with previous mix
+ White.

3. Add detail lines on legs and
toenails with Raw Umber,
slightly thinned, using the round
brush.

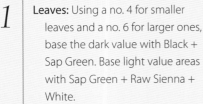

1 **Leaves:** Using a no. 4 for smaller leaves and a no. 6 for larger ones, base the dark value with Black + Sap Green. Base light value areas with Sap Green + Raw Sienna + White.

Blossoms: Base the dark value with Alizarin Crimson + Raw Sienna and the light value with the same mix + White, using the no. 2 or no. 4 bright.

Branch: Base the dark value with Burnt Sienna + Raw Umber and the light value with Raw Sienna, using the no. 4.

2 **Leaves:** Blend between values, with the growth direction, using the chisel edge of the brush. Lay in highlights using the light value mix + more White.

Blossoms: Blend between values, following the growth direction of each petal. Highlight with White + Cadmium Yellow Pale on over-lapping petals and at some outer edges. Base the dark centers loose-ly with a mix of Alizarin Crimson + Black, using the no. 2.

Branch: Blend where the values meet, and highlight within upper half of branch with Raw Sienna + White.

3 **Leaves:** Blend the highlights again with growth direction. Add central vein structure with chisel edge, using the light value green mix. Accent with Alizarin Crimson + Raw Sienna in a few places. Blend to soften.

Blossoms: Blend highlighting to fol-low growth direction. Highlight with pure White in a few places. Add center detail lines with strokes of slightly-thinned White + a bit of Alizarin Crimson + Raw Sienna mix. Add dots of White.

Finish: Before painting is dry, clean up any graphite lines or messy edges with the no. 8 bright dipped in odorless thinner and blotted on a paper towel.

Sherry C. Nelson

Variegated Fairy Wren

BACKGROUND PREPARATION

Surface:
9" x 12" (23cm × 30cm)
hardboard panel,
1/8" (3mm) thick

Delta Ceramcoat
acrylic paints:
Moss Green
Gamal Green
Seminole Green
Flesh Tan

FOR PROJECT

Winsor & Newton
Artists' Oils:
Ivory Black
Titanium White
Raw Sienna
Raw Umber
Burnt Sienna
Sap Green
Cadmium Yellow Pale
French Ultramarine
Winsor Red

Brushes:
nos. 2, 4, 6, 8 red sable
  brights
no. 0 red sable round

THE FAIRY WRENS are native to Australia and New Guinea and are an ancient family whose relationship with other species is not clear. But we do know they are much loved. The rich blue plumage and perky behavior—dashing through the bushes and shrubs with tails cocked—have endeared them to birders and non-birders alike. When their nest is threatened, the bird often leads the intruder away, scuttling along the ground in a unique posture called the "rodent-run" display. To see a Fairy Wren was my fondest hope when I went to Australia to teach. What a delight to spot a whole family of them at the Botanical Gardens on the Sydney waterfront!

Black + Raw Umber

White + Raw Sienna

Raw Sienna + Raw Umber

Burnt Sienna + Winsor Red

White + Raw Umber

White + French Ultramarine

Burnt Sienna + Raw Sienna

Burnt Sienna + Raw Sienna + White

Raw Sienna + Raw Umber

Cadmium Yellow Pale + Raw Sienna

White + Cadmium Yellow Pale

Black + Sap Green

White + Sap Green + French Ultramarine

Previous mix + White

Alizarin Crimson + French Ultramarine

Line Drawing

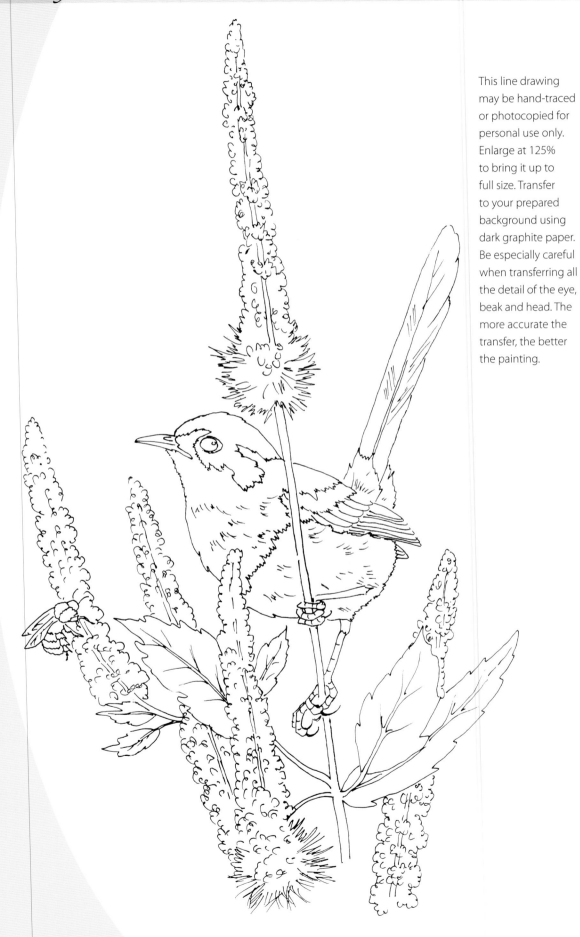

This line drawing may be hand-traced or photocopied for personal use only. Enlarge at 125% to bring it up to full size. Transfer to your prepared background using dark graphite paper. Be especially careful when transferring all the detail of the eye, beak and head. The more accurate the transfer, the better the painting.

Field Sketches

A garden flower such as this dramatic Veronica may be found in many different parts of the world. Taking floral reference photos where you see birds helps provide valuable information when choosing floral elements for future paintings you wish to be characteristic of a particular bird's country or habitat.

SUPERB FAIRY WREN
Another of Australia's nine species of Fairy Wren, this one's range is limited to the Southeastern part of the country. Fairy Wrens live in a communal family group, with a dominant pair nesting and laying eggs each year. Other family members—aunts, uncles, or the young siblings from the previous year— help with raising and protecting the young, increasing the survival rate dramatically.

Tail Feathers

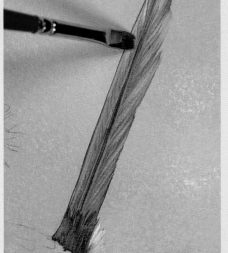

PREPARE THE BACKGROUND

Base the hardboard panel, using a sponge roller, with Moss Green. Let dry. Sand well. Rebase, and while wet, drizzle on a 2-inch (51mm) stripe of Tide Pool Blue in two different places on the surface. Use the same roller to blend blue softly here and there into basecoat. Now add a little Light Ivory in the center of the surface, again blending and moving color around to achieve nice value gradations between the splotches of Ivory and the background. Let dry, sand well, and spray with Liberty Matte Finish. Refer to the chapter on Preparing the Background for additional information on surface preparation.

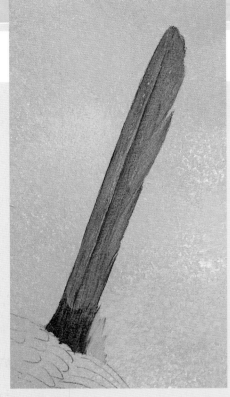

1 **Tail:** Using a no. 4 bright, base blue feathers with French Ultramarine.
Undertail Coverts: Base with Raw Sienna + White, using the no. 2.
Uppertail Coverts: Base with Black + Raw Umber, using the no. 2.

2 **Tail:** Streak in feather lines with White on the chisel edge of the brush following lateral growth direction. Lightest areas should be toward tail tip and right side of tail. Lay in central shaft line with Black + Raw Umber.
Undertail Coverts: Highlight with White.
Uppertail Coverts: Highlight with Raw Sienna.

3 **Tail:** Note how directional lines on tail feathers are very close together.
Undertail Coverts: Blend highlight with choppy strokes of the no. 2, following the growth direction of the feathers. Do the same for the uppertail coverts.

Wing, Belly and Breast

1

Primaries: Base with Raw Umber using the no. 4. Mark in feather lines with stylus as you cover them with paint.

Greater Coverts: Base with Raw Sienna + Raw Umber using the no. 2. Use stylus to mark in feather lines.

Median Coverts: Base with Burnt Sienna + Winsor Red, using the no. 2.

Scapulars: Base with French Ultramarine, using the no. 2.

Belly: Base dark value with Raw Sienna. Base light value with White, using the no. 4.

Breast: Base with Black + Raw Umber, using the no. 4.

2

Primaries: Streak in feather lines using chisel edge and White + Raw Sienna.

Greater Coverts: Streak in feather lines using chisel edge and White + Raw Sienna.

Median Coverts: Chop in a few short markings to indicate feathers using Raw Sienna + White.

Scapulars: Chop in short feather markings using French Ultramarine + White.

Belly: Blend between values, creating a choppy, directional, feathery look. Highlight with White.

Breast: Highlight with Raw Sienna. Use choppy short strokes of the chisel and follow growth direction of the feathers and create form and shape.

3

Median Coverts: Blend choppy feather strokes to soften, to make them more realistic.

Scapulars: Blend feather strokes to soften. Fluff a few strokes over Median Coverts to give a fluffy appearance.

Belly: Blend with short, choppy strokes of the chisel at edges of highlight values, gradually creating a final value gradation to give the shape and form of the bird's body. Be cautious with growth direction.

Breast: Finalize blending with a few directional strokes. Don't overwork; you'll get mud.

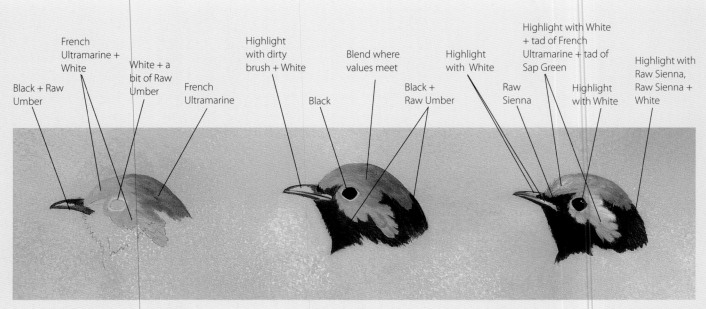

French
Ultramarine +
White

White + a
bit of Raw
Umber

Black + Raw
Umber

French
Ultramarine

Highlight
with dirty
brush + White

Blend where
values meet

Black

Highlight
with White

Black +
Raw Umber

Highlight with White
+ tad of French
Ultramarine + tad of
Sap Green

Raw
Sienna

Highlight
with White

Highlight with
Raw Sienna,
Raw Sienna +
White

1. Paint the eye-ring first, using the round brush for the eye detail. Use the no. 2 bright to paint the other head areas.

2. Base eye with Black. Base remaining areas as shown.

3. Highlight eye with White dot using round brush. Blend the beak where values meet. Rehighlight beak with White if needed. Highlight forehead and crown with White + a bit of French Ultramarine + a bit of Sap Green. Highlight at nape with Raw Sienna first, then Raw Sienna + White. Highlight throat with Raw Sienna.

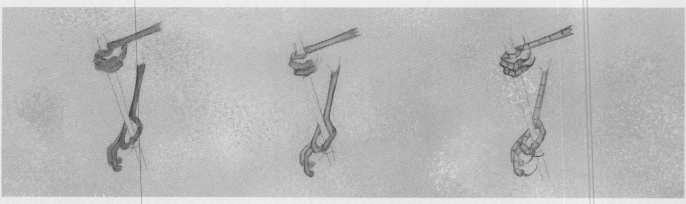

1. Base with Burnt Sienna + Raw Sienna, using the no. 2 bright.

2. Highlight with dirty brush + White.

3. Add detail lines on legs with Raw Umber, slightly thinned, using the round brush. Do toe-nails with slightly-thinned Raw Umber.

Veronica and Carpenter Bee

1
Leaves: Using a no. 4 for smaller leaves and a no. 6 for larger ones, base the dark value with Black + Sap Green. Base light value areas with White + Sap Green + French Ultramarine.

Stems: Base wider stems with same mixes used for leaves, using the no. 2. For small stems, just base with Black + Sap Green.

Blossoms: Base the interior stalk of the bloom with Black + Raw Umber. Add dabs of same mix along stalk to indicate the tiny calyxes that hold each little individual blossom.

2
Leaves: Blend between values, with the growth direction, using the chisel edge of the brush. Lay in highlight areas using the light value mix + more White.

Stems: Highlight down center of each small stem with same light value mix used for leaves.

Blossoms: Using the flattened tip of the round brush, stipple on a dark base color of Alizarin Crimson + French Ultramarine. At bottom of larger blossoms, thin the mix slightly, and stroke fine lines in a rough sunburst where flower is fully bloomed out.

3
Leaves: Blend the highlights. Add central vein structure with chisel edge, using the light value green mix.

Stems: Do any final blending needed.

Blossoms: Add white to purple mix used for base color and stipple to create highlights on each blossom, primarily on outer edges and at the top of the spike.

Finish: Before painting is dry, clean up any graphite lines or messy edges with the no. 8 bright dipped in odorless thinner and blotted on a paper towel.

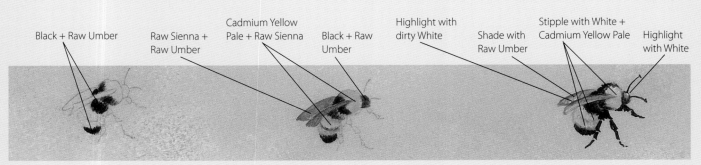

Black + Raw Umber

Raw Sienna + Raw Umber

Cadmium Yellow Pale + Raw Sienna

Black + Raw Umber

Highlight with dirty White

Shade with Raw Umber

Stipple with White + Cadmium Yellow Pale

Highlight with White

1. Base dark areas with Black + Raw Umber, using the no. 0 bright.

2. Base wings with Raw Sienna + Raw Umber. Base yellow areas with Cadmium Yellow Pale + Raw Sienna. Base head with Black + Raw Umber.

3. Shade along edges of wings with Raw Umber. Highlight with dirty White on wings and head. Stipple yellow areas with White + Cadmium Yellow Pale highlight. Detail legs and antennae with Black.

Sherry C. Nelson

Magnolia Warbler

BACKGROUND PREPARATION

Surface:
9" x 12" (23cm x 30cm)
hardboard panel, ⅛"
(3mm) thick

*Delta Ceramcoat
acrylic paints:*
Moss Green
Seminole Green
Gamal Green
Light Ivory

FOR PROJECT

*Winsor & Newton
Artists' Oils:*
Ivory Black
Titanium White
Raw Sienna
Raw Umber
Burnt Sienna
Sap Green
Cadmium Yellow Pale
Winsor Red

Brushes:
nos. 2, 4, 6, 8 red sable
 brights
no. 0 red sable round

 BLOSSOMING TREES ARE OFTEN OVERLOOKED by painters, yet make a lovely setting for a beautiful bird. This is a branch of Tecoma stans or Yellow Elder. The Magnolia Warbler I chose for this painting is one of some 44 species of Wood Warblers found in North America, most of which are not commonly seen because they often forage high in the tree canopy, are quick and active, and of course, small enough to hide behind almost any leaf. But warblers are varied and exquisite little birds, well worth the time to watch and study—and paint!

Black + Raw Umber

Black + Raw Umber + White

White + Raw Umber + Black

Cadmium Yellow Pale + Winsor Red

Cadmium Yellow Pale + White

Burnt Sienna + Raw Umber

Black + Sap Green

Sap Green + Raw Sienna + White

Sap Green + Raw Sienna + more White

Cadmium Yellow Pale + Raw Sienna

White + Cadmium Yellow Pale

This line drawing may be hand-traced or photocopied for personal use only. Enlarge at 111% to bring it up to full size. Transfer to your prepared background using dark graphite paper. Be especially careful when transferring all the detail of the eye, beak and head. The more accurate the transfer, the better the painting.

Field Sketches

This lovely "butterfly of the bird world" is found primarily in eastern North America, and nests in mixed coniferous woodlands. It's hard to get good reference photos of warblers because they are active and generally found high in the trees. A great photo to paint from.

YELLOW-RUMPED WARBLER

This beautiful little bird is the only warbler regularly seen in the winter in North America. It can survive in part because it can digest the hard waxy coating on bayberries, thus managing even when there are no insects to be found.

KENTUCKY WARBLER

The Kentucky Warbler is a bird of the thickets and forest understory. It winters in Central America where forest destruction is ongoing and thus threatens the continued survival of this beautiful bird.

YELLOW WARBLER

A widely recognized warbler and one that's not shy, the Yellow is commonly found in gardens and dooryards. The rusty streaks on the breast are diagnostic. Most warblers migrate in flocks at night, and communicate with each other with buzzy or lisping flight calls.

Tail, Wing and Breast

 PREPARE THE BACKGROUND

Base the hardboard panel, using a sponge roller, with Moss Green. Let dry, sand well. Rebase, and while wet, drizzle on a 1-inch (25mm) stripe of Seminole Green at the edge of the surface in two places. Blend this green into the basecoat with the same roller.

Next add a little Gamal Green within the previous green areas, again blending to achieve nice value gradations between the added greens and the background. Finally drizzle a little Flesh Tan in the central area of the surface and blend it here and there into the background. Let dry, sand well, and spray with Liberty Matte Finish. Refer to the Preparing the Background chapter for additional information on surface preparation.

1 **Tail:** Using a no. 4 bright, base dark upper half with Black + Raw Umber. Base rest of tail with the same mix + a little White to gray.
Primaries: Base with Black + Raw Umber using the no. 4 bright. Draw in feather lines with stylus.
Wing Coverts: Base with White, using the no. 2.
Scapulars: Base with Black + Raw Umber, using the no. 2.
Undertail Coverts: Base with White, using the no. 2.
Breast: Base with Cadmium Yellow Pale + a little Winsor Red, using the no. 4. Carefully avoid covering the markings.

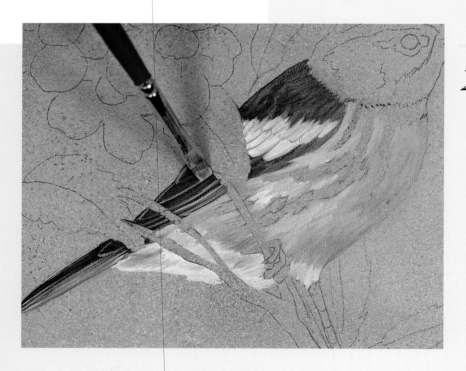

2 **Tail:** Streak in feather lines with dirty White on the chisel edge of the brush.
Primaries: Streak in feather lines with dirty White on the chisel edge of the brush.
Wing Coverts: Indicate separation between individual feathers with Black + Raw Umber lines. Highlight tips of nearer covert feathers with White.
Scapulars: Highlight with dirty white, chopping in a few rough markings to indicate small rows of feathers at bottom of area.
Undertail Coverts: Shade with Raw Umber.
Breast: Shade with Burnt Sienna, and in darker areas, with Burnt Sienna + Raw Umber. Highlight with Cadmium Yellow Pale + White.

Wing, Breast and Head

1

Scapulars: Strengthen highlight in scapulars with a few choppy strokes of the brush using cleaner White.

Undertail Coverts: Blend shading with choppy strokes of the no. 2, following the growth direction. Blend where undertail feathers meet breast feathers; fluff areas together with chisel strokes.

Breast: Blend shading to soften, following growth direction and using short strokes. Blend highlights as well, being careful to avoid markings. Rehighlight with White if desired before adding markings.

Markings: Base carefully with Black + Raw Umber, using the no. 2. Do not allow dark mix to blend into the yellow. Use the brush's chisel edge to zig-zag markings here and there along edges to connect the colors. If you begin carrying color, stop, wipe the brush, and reload before continuing.

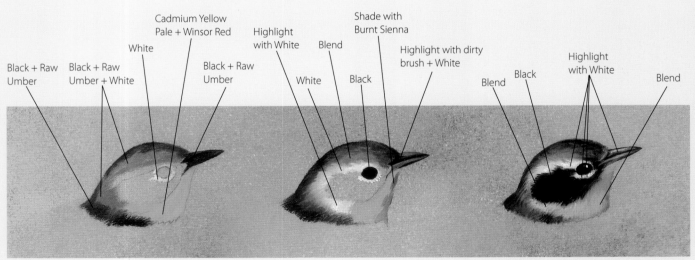

1. Paint the eye-ring with White, using the round brush. Base nape, top of crown and beak with Black + Raw Umber, using the no. 2. Base lighter value on crown area with Black + Raw Umber + White. Base throat with Cadmium Yellow Pale + Winsor Red.

2. Base eye with Black. Blend between crown values with growth direction. Base eyebrow stripe with White and blend carefully into edge of gray crown area. Highlight beak with dirty White. Shade throat with Burnt Sienna. Highlight side of throat with White.

3. Highlight eye with White dot using round brush. Blend the beak where values meet. Re-highlight beak with White if needed. Highlight eyebrow and wider portion of eye-ring under eye with White. Blend shading and highlights on throat, following growth direction and using very short strokes. Base auricular with Black. Connect with zig-zag chisel work to feather areas around it.

Feet and Honey Bee

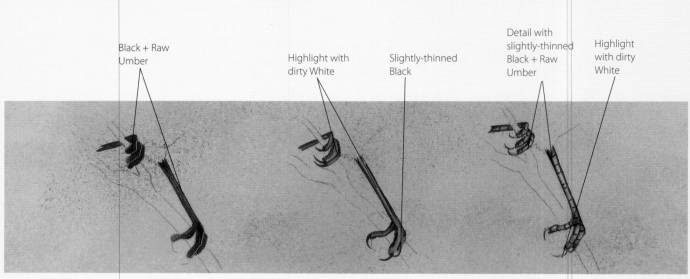

Black + Raw Umber

Highlight with dirty White

Slightly-thinned Black

Detail with slightly-thinned Black + Raw Umber

Highlight with dirty White

1. Base with Black + Raw Umber, using the no. 2 bright.

2. Highlight with dirty brush + White. Use slightly-thinned Black and round brush for toenails.

3. Add detail lines on legs with Black + Raw Umber, slightly thinned, using the round brush. Highlight toenails with a bit of dirty White.

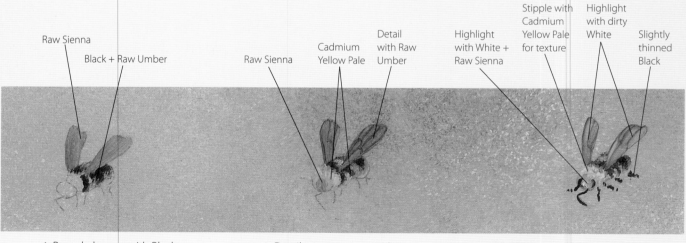

Raw Sienna

Black + Raw Umber

Raw Sienna

Cadmium Yellow Pale

Detail with Raw Umber

Highlight with White + Raw Sienna

Stipple with Cadmium Yellow Pale for texture

Highlight with dirty White

Slightly thinned Black

1. Base dark areas with Black + Raw Umber, using the no. 0 bright. Base wings with sparse Raw Sienna.

2. Detail wing sections with slightly thinned Raw Umber. Base yellow areas with Cadmium Yellow Pale. Base head with Raw Sienna.

3. Highlight with dirty White on wings and head. Stipple yellow areas with Cadmium Yellow Pale highlight. Highlight head with dirty White. Detail legs and antennae with Black.

Leaves, Blossoms and Final Blending

1

Leaves: Using a no. 4 for smaller leaves and a no. 6 for larger ones, base the dark value with Black + Sap Green. Base light value areas with Sap Green + Raw Sienna + White.

Stems and Calyxes: Base wider stems with same mixes used for leaves, using the no. 2. For small stems and calyxes, base entirely with Black + Sap Green.

Blossoms: Base with Cadmium Yellow Pale + Raw Sienna.

Buds: Base with Cadmium Yellow Pale + Raw Sienna.

2

Leaves: Blend between values, with the growth direction, using the chisel edge of the brush. Lay in highlight areas using the light value mix + more White.

Stems and Calyxes: Highlight down center of each small stem with same light value mix used for leaves. Highlight calyxes with same mix.

Blossoms: Shade with Burnt Sienna in curving shape at center of each bloom. Highlight with White on overlapping petals and at some outer edges.

Buds: Shade with a little dark green mix. Highlight with White.

3

Leaves: Blend the highlights. Add central vein structure with chisel edge, using the light value green mix. Accent with Raw Sienna on some leaves and Burnt Sienna on others. Blend to soften.

Stems and Calyxes: Do any final blending needed.

Blossoms: Soften Burnt Sienna shading by pulling outward from center following growth direction of petals. Blend highlighting to follow growth direction as well. Accent with a little strong orange made with Cadmium Yellow Pale + a bit more Winsor Red than used for the base mix. Add center detail strokes with White + a bit of basecoat yellow mix.

Buds: Blend shading and highlights. Accent with orangey mix as for flowers.

Finish: Before painting is dry, clean up any graphite lines or messy edges with the no. 8 bright dipped in odorless thinner and blotted on a paper towel.

Sherry C. Nelson

Wood Thrush

BACKGROUND PREPARATION

Surface:
9" x 12" (23cm x 30cm) hardboard panel, ⅛" (3mm) thick

Delta Ceramcoat acrylic paints:
Moss Green
Antique Rose
Desert Sun Orange
Light Ivory

FOR PROJECT

Winsor & Newton Artists' Oils:
Ivory Black
Titanium White
Raw Sienna
Raw Umber
Burnt Sienna
Sap Green
Alizarin Crimson
French Ultramarine

Brushes:
nos. 2, 4, 6, 8 red sable brights
no. 0 red sable round

THE SUBTLE, SUBDUED PLUMAGE of the lovely Wood Thrush belies the glory of its song. The intricate, flute-like medley of notes is one of the most complex in the bird world and one of the most spectacular. Sadly, these wonderful birds are losing ground to Brown-headed Cowbird parasitism and to loss of habitat both here and in their Central American wintering grounds. The female lays three to four beautiful glossy eggs, as blue as the American Robin's, a close cousin.

Raw Sienna + White

Burnt Sienna + Raw Sienna

Black + Raw Umber

White + Raw Umber + Black

Burnt Sienna + White

Black + Sap Green

Sap Green + Raw Sienna + White

White + Sap Green + Raw Sienna

More White + Sap Green + Raw Sienna

Alizarin Crimson + French Ultramarine + Raw Umber

Previous mix + White

This line drawing may be hand-traced or photocopied for personal use only. Enlarge at 111% to bring it up to full size. Transfer to your prepared background using dark graphite paper. Be especially careful when transferring all the detail of the eye, beak and head. The more accurate the transfer, the better the painting.

Field Sketches

In this shot, the bird is caught in an alert pose, with orangey head feathers crested.

Here, well, why wouldn't the bird seem more relaxed? Check out the reflection of the spotted breast in the "bathwater." Both shots show the wonderful Burnt Sienna accent glowing on the head. We'll strive for that in the painting, but we'll leave out the pink berry stains on the face and breast.

HERMIT THRUSH

The Hermit is our common backyard thrush here in Arizona and in much of North America as well. It comes to our water drip, hangs on the end of the hose nozzle, and drinks right out of the spout. Paler than the Wood Thrush, the Hermit shares similar habits and has an ethereal, fluting song. They mostly winter here, so we rarely get the pleasure of hearing them sing.

Tail and Wing

PREPARE THE BACKGROUND

Base the hardboard panel, using a sponge roller, with Moss Green. Let dry, sand well. Rebase, and while wet, drizzle on a 1-inch (25mm) stripe of Desert Sun Orange and a 2-inch (51mm) stripe of Antique Rose side by side near the edge of the surface. Blend into the basecoat with the same roller, moving colors here and there primarily around the edges of the surface to distribute the color and soften into the background.

Then, in the center of the surface, drizzle 1 to 2 inches (25 to 51mm) of Flesh Tan. Blend here and there to distribute this highlight and to intermingle with the rose tones. Let dry, sand well, and spray with Liberty Matte Finish. Refer to the Preparing the Background chapter for additional information on surface preparation.

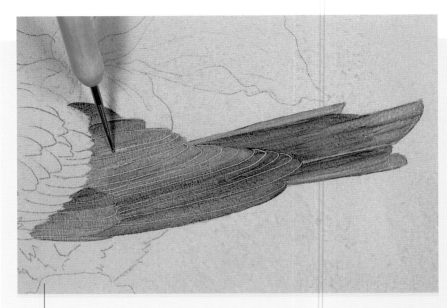

1 **Tail:** Using a no. 4 or no. 6 bright, base dark value with Raw Umber. Base light value with Raw Sienna.

Primaries and Secondaries: Using the no. 4, base dark feather areas with Raw Umber and lighter feathers with Raw Sienna; draw in feather lines with a stylus as you cover them.

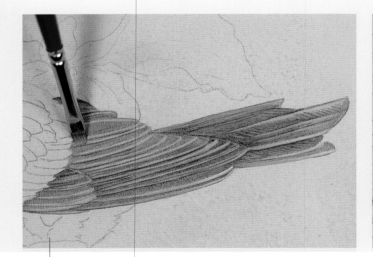

2 **Tail:** Blend lengthwise, where values meet. Lay on feather lines with Raw Sienna + White. With a dry brush, reblend a few of the tail feathers with the lateral growth direction, using very close-together chisel lines to suggest a more realistic feathered appearance.

Primaries and Secondaries: Lay in feather edge lines with Raw Sienna + White. Reset growth direction on a few of the wider top feathers using the close-together chisel edge lines the same as for the tail.

3 **Tail:** Accent with a little Burnt Sienna + Raw Sienna between some of the feather lines.

Primaries and Secondaries: Accent with the Burnt Sienna + Raw Sienna mix between some of the feather lines, particularly at the base of the feathers where the shadow would be a bit darker.

Wing and Breast

1 **Coverts and Scapulars:** Using the no. 4, base the dark area with Raw Umber and the light value with Raw Sienna. Draw in covert feather lines with the stylus as you base over them.

Breast and Belly: Using the no. 4, base the dark value with Raw Sienna + Burnt Sienna and the light value area sparsely with White. Begin creating growth direction as you lay the color on, even at this early stage.

2 **Coverts and Scapulars:** Blend where the values meet, with the growth direction. Then add feather lines with Raw Sienna + White, using the chisel edge of the no. 2 and beginning with the bottom row. As feather edge lines are completed, add central shaft lines on a few feathers with the same mix. Chop some shorter, more indistinct rows of feathers above the defined coverts to make a gradation of detail as you move up the wing.

Breast and Belly: Blend where values meet. Use choppy short strokes of the chisel and follow growth direction of the feathers and create form and shape. Think texture! Shade next to wing and outer edge of body with Raw Umber. Highlight in lightest part of breast with more White.

3 **Breast:** Use short strokes of the chisel, following the growth direction, to blend where the values meet in both shading and highlight areas. Flip up a few soft feathers from breast over the edge of the wing.

Center the tracing paper overlay from your original transfer over the painting, being careful not to move it around too much. Using the ballpoint pen, retransfer the breast spots with firm pressure.

4 **Breast:** Using the round brush, add the breast spots with slightly-thinned Black + Raw Umber for the darker ones and the same mix + a little White for the grayer spots next to the wing.

Head

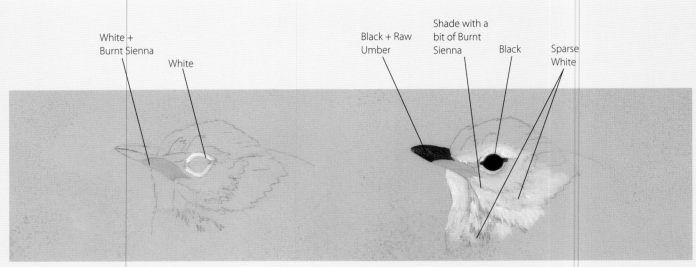

White +
Burnt Sienna

White

Black + Raw
Umber

Shade with a
bit of Burnt
Sienna

Black

Sparse
White

1. Using the round brush, base the eye-ring with White. Base the pink area of the beak with White + Burnt Sienna using the no. 2.

2. Base eye with Black using the round brush. Base rest of beak with Black + Raw Umber using the no. 2. Base light areas with sparse White. Shade above and below eye with a little bit of Burnt Sienna.

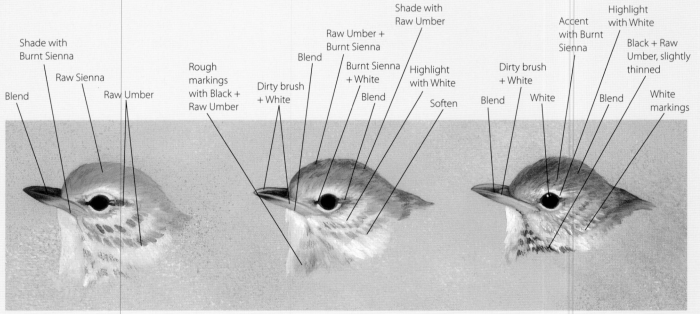

Shade with
Burnt Sienna

Raw Sienna

Blend

Raw Umber

Rough
markings
with Black +
Raw Umber

Dirty brush
+ White

Blend

Raw Umber +
Burnt Sienna

Shade with
Raw Umber

Burnt Sienna
+ White

Blend

Highlight
with White

Soften

Dirty brush
+ White

Blend

White

Accent
with Burnt
Sienna

Highlight
with White

Black + Raw
Umber, slightly
thinned

Blend

White
markings

3. Blend the beak where values meet. Shade with a little Burnt Sienna at the edge of the lower mandible. Base the crown with Raw Sienna. Base the eyeline with Raw Umber. Establish initial markings on auricular with short strokes of Raw Umber.

4. Highlight the beak with dirty White. Shade the crown with Raw Umber + Burnt Sienna. Blend the eyeline into surrounding White. Add faint curving lines of Burnt Sienna + White inside eye to cut off the "corners." Shade at the nape with Raw Umber. Blend shading on beak. Soften auricular markings. Highlight between markings with more White. Add rough markings on throat with Black + Raw Umber.

5. Highlight eye with White dot using round brush. Highlight with White above the eye. Blend highlight on beak, and rehighlight with more White if needed. Accent crown strongly with Burnt Sienna. Blend to soften shading on crown. Use the round brush to add tiny white markings in between the dark markings on the auricular. Add more defined dark markings on throat using slightly thinned Black + Raw Umber on the round brush.

Leaves and Flowers

1 **Leaves and Stems:** Using a no. 4 for smaller areas and a no. 6 for the larger ones, base the dark value with Black + Sap Green. Base the light value with Sap Green + Raw Sienna + White.

Green Sepals: Using the no. 2, base with White + Sap Green + a little Raw Sienna.

Magenta Petals: Using the no. 2, base the petals with a mix of Alizarin Crimson + a little French Ultramarine + a little Raw Umber.

2 **Leaves and Stems:** Blend where values meet, following the natural growth direction of the leaves. Highlight leaves with White + Sap Green + Raw Sienna. Use the same mix to highlight down center of each stem.

Sepals: Accent with a a bit of Sap Green. Highlight with White.

Petals: Highlight in central area of each petal with the magenta petal base mix + White.

3 **Leaves:** Blend the leaf highlights. Add off-white flip turns with palest light green mix. Add veining with light green mix using the chisel edge of the brush.

Sepals: Blend first the accents and then the highlights with the growth direction of each sepal. Streak in faint veining with Sap Green using the chisel edge.

Petals: Blend highlights with growth direction where values meet.

4 **Flower Details:** Using the round brush, add fine, irregular veining within each magenta petal using a slightly thinned mix of Alizarin Crimson + French Ultramarine + Raw Umber. With the round brush, tap in a small circle of White for the flower center. Fill it in with the magenta petal base mix. Add detail markings and lines at the base of the lip using slightly thinned White and the round brush.

Finish: Before painting is dry, clean up any graphite lines or messy edges with the no. 8 bright dipped in odorless thinner and blotted on a paper towel.

Sherry C. Nelson

Green Jay

BACKGROUND PREPARATION

Surface:
11" x 14" (28cm x 36cm) hardboard panel, 1/8" (3mm) thick

Delta Ceramcoat acrylic paints:
Moss Green
Tide Pool Blue
Light Ivory

FOR PROJECT

Winsor & Newton Artists' Oils:
Ivory Black
Titanium White
Raw Sienna
Raw Umber
Burnt Sienna
Sap Green
Cadmium Yellow Pale
Alizarin Crimson
French Ultramarine

Brushes:
nos. 2, 4, 6, 8 red sable brights
no. 0 red sable round

MIGRATE TO THE LOWER RIO GRANDE VALLEY with the rest of the Winter Texans, camp in one of the many RV parks, and invite this gorgeous, exotic-looking jay to your feeder! Besides the Green Jay, which is actually quite common in its restricted range, South Texas hosts numerous species found nowhere else in North America. Bring your binoculars and investigate the string of refuges called the Great Texas Birding Trail—you'll see some of the most beautiful of North American birds.

Black + French Ultramarine

French Ultramarine + Titanium White

White + French Ultramarine

Cadmium Yellow Pale + Raw Sienna

Cadmium Yellow Pale + White

White + Sap Green + Raw Sienna

French Ultramarine + Sap Green

Raw Sienna + Raw Umber

More White + Sap Green + Raw Sienna

Black + Sap Green

Raw Sienna + White

Alizarin Crimson + Burnt Sienna

Alizarin Crimson + Raw Sienna

Black + Raw Umber

French Ultramarine + Raw Umber

Line Drawing

This line drawing may be hand-traced or photo-copied for personal use only. Enlarge at 125% to bring it up to full size. Transfer to your prepared background using dark graphite paper. Be especially careful when transferring all the detail of the eye, beak and head. The more accurate the transfer, the better the painting.

Field Sketches

CLARK'S NUTCRACKER

An unusual member of the Jay family, the very pale gray, black and white Clark's Nutcracker has a chisel-like beak, which is adapted for opening pine cones to reach the seeds. Found in the coniferous forests of the West, it is highly dependent on pine cones for food, and will fly long distances to find a reliable food source.

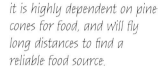

Formally called the Rio Grande Jay, this bird nests in dense thickets of thorny brush. In winter it favors ebony seeds and the Texas palmetto fruit for food. Solitary nesters, the Green Jays can be seen in small flocks outside of breeding season. The Green Jay in my painting is shown with the Paradise Poinciana, an arid country plant that's not a native species, but now can be found in the same thorn scrub habitat characteristic of the jay.

MAGPIE JAY

The Magpie Jay is a tropical species normally found in Central America and Mexico, but who occasionally visits the borders of southern Arizona. A large, noisy and aggressive bird, it will mob human intruders during nesting season.

Tail Feathers

PREPARE THE BACKGROUND

Base the hardboard panel, using a sponge roller, with Moss Green. Let dry. Sand well. Rebase, and while wet, drizzle on a 2-inch (51mm) stripe of Tide Pool Blue in two different places on the surface. Use the same roller to blend blue softly here and there into the basecoat. Now add a little Light Ivory in the center of the surface, again blending and moving color around to achieve nice value gradations between the splotches of Ivory and the background. Let dry, sand well, and spray with Liberty Matte Finish. Refer to the Preparing the Background chapter for additional information on surface preparation.

1 **Tail:** Using a no. 4 or no. 6, base dark blue value with Black + French Ultramarine and the medium value blue with French Ultramarine + White. Base light value blue with White + French Ultramarine. Base yellow edge with Cadmium Yellow Pale + Raw Sienna. At this stage there is no growth direction established.

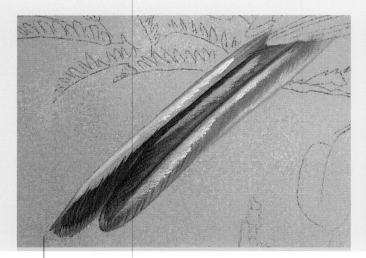

2 **Tail:** Blend the edge of the yellow areas into the adjacent blue feather, following the lateral growth direction, with a series of close together lines. With a dirty blue brush, begin to establish the lateral growth directions on the other feathers as well, using the chisel edge and laying in close together lines to create feather fiber. Note that the directions change with the area of tail you are working.

Apply White highlights on the three blue feather areas and Cadmium Yellow Pale + White highlights at edge of yellow feather.

3 **Tail:** Reblend to achieve final growth direction and fiber texture in each area of the tail. Strengthen the darkest blues with a pure French Ultramarine accent.

Wing, Belly and Breast

1 **Wing:** Using the no. 4, base the primary feathers with French Ultramarine + Sap Green + a tiny bit of White. Base the lighter secondary sections with the same mix + more White.

Coverts: Using the no. 4, base with same mix as for secondaries. Draw in stylus lines if desired to establish feather location.

Back: Using the no. 4 or no. 6, base the back with White + Raw Sienna + Sap Green, a very pale mix.

Undertail Coverts: Using the no. 4, base with Cadmium Yellow Pale + White.

Breast: Using the no. 4, base the dark value with Raw Umber + Raw Sienna. Use White + Sap Green + Raw Sienna for the medium value, and White + Cadmium Yellow Pale for the lightest value.

2 **Wing:** Separate the primary wing feathers with dark lines of Black + Sap Green. Streak the secondary feathers with Black + Sap Green, and then with some French Ultramarine + White.

Coverts: Edge covert feathers with French Ultramarine + White, using the no. 4 or no. 2. Add a few central shaft lines.

Back: Shade with a mix of Sap Green + French Ultramarine. Highlight with Sap Green + Raw Sienna + White.

Breast: Blend between values, then highlight with a pale mix of White + Cadmium Yellow Pale.

3 **Wing:** Highlight tips of primaries between dark lines using Raw Sienna + White. Highlight central portions of primary feather edges by streaking with White + Sap Green + a bit of French Ultramarine avoiding the dark shadow lines.

Back: Soften shading and highlights, working to create form and shape with soft strokes of the chisel edge of the brush. The overall look of Green Jay plumage is sleek with poorly defined feathering.

Breast: Use the chisel with more vigor here, blending the edges of the highlight, creating texture and growth direction. Flip a few soft strokes over the edges of the wing to soften.

Head and Feet

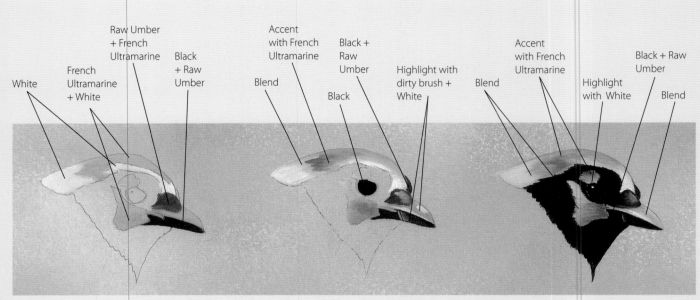

White

Raw Umber + French Ultramarine

French Ultramarine + White

Black + Raw Umber

Accent with French Ultramarine

Blend

Black + Raw Umber

Black

Highlight with dirty brush + White

Accent with French Ultramarine

Blend

Black + Raw Umber

Highlight with White

Blend

1. Do eye and eye detail with the round brush. Use the no. 2 for rest of head area. Base the eye-ring with Raw Umber + White. Base the white areas with White. Base the light blue areas with French Ultramarine + White. Base cere behind beak with Raw Umber + French Ultramarine. Base lower mandible with Black + Raw Umber.

2. Base eye with Black. Blend between values on crown. Accent crown and auricular with French Ultramarine. Base dark area above beak with Black + Raw Umber. Highlight beak, cere, and lower mandible with dirty brush + White.

3. Highlight eye with dot of White. Blend accents on crown and auricular to a gradation. Accent blue spot above eye with a bit of French Ultramarine. Blend the smaller areas of highlights to soften. Base remainder of head with Black + Raw Umber. Use chisel edge to slightly connect dark areas to surrounding head colors. Establish growth direction as you work. Do not blend; colors on bird's head remain very distinct.

Black + Raw Umber

Highlight with dirty brush + White.

Detail lines, toenails with Black + Raw Umber, slightly thinned

1. Base with Black + Raw Umber, using the no. 2 bright.

2. Highlight with dirty brush + White.

3. Add detail lines and toenails with Black + Raw Umber, slightly thinned, using the round brush.

Leaves and Flower

1

Stamens: Using the no. 4, base the dark value with Alizarin Crimson and the light with Winsor Red.

Stems: Using the no. 2 bright, base the leaf stems with Black + Sap Green.

Branch: Base dark value with Black + Sap Green, using the no. 6. Base the lighter value with Sap Green + Raw Sienna + White.

Leaflets: Using a no. 0 bright, base darker leaflets with the dark value of Black + Sap Green and the lighter with Sap Green + Raw Sienna + White.

Flower and Flower Stems: Base dark value with Black + Sap Green. Base the light value with Cadmium Yellow Pale + Raw Sienna, using the no. 2 bright for smaller buds and the no. 4 for larger ones.

2

Stamens: Blend where values meet. Highlight with dirty brush + White.

Stems: Highlight with light green mix.

Branch: Blend to connect values, then chop in light value with Cadmium Yellow Pale + Raw Sienna.

Leaflets: Highlight most with a lighter green mix of Sap Green + Raw Sienna + White or a mix of French Ultramarine + White.

Flower and Flower Stems: Blend where values meet, then highlight with Cadmium Yellow Pale + White.

3

Stamens: Blend slightly where values meet.

Stems: Accent some stems with Alizarin Crimson + Burnt Sienna.

Branch: Chop values together with chisel edge of the brush to create realistic texture. Accent some areas with Alizarin Crimson + Burnt Sienna.

Leaflets: Blend highlights if necessary.

Flower and Flower Stems: Blend between values to create gradation within each bud. Shade with additional dark green mix if needed. Re-highlight with White on dominant bud tips, stippling White with the flattened tip of the round brush for a little texture. Accent some of the flower stems and the sides of some of the buds with a little Alizarin Crimson + Raw Sienna. Add the tiny calyxes between buds with Alizarin Crimson + Raw Sienna, using the no. 0 bright. Highlight each with a little dirty brush + White.

Finish: Before painting is dry, clean up any graphite lines or messy edges with the no. 8 bright dipped in odorless thinner and blotted on a paper towel.

Sherry C. Nelson

American Robin

BACKGROUND PREPARATION

Surface:
9" x 12" (23cm x 30cm)
hardboard panel, ⅛"
(3mm) thick

*Delta Ceramcoat
acrylic paints:*
Moss Green
Desert Sun Orange
Light Ivory
Flesh Tan

FOR PROJECT

*Winsor & Newton
Artists' Oils:*
Ivory Black
Titanium White
Raw Sienna
Raw Umber
Burnt Sienna
Sap Green
Cadmium Yellow Pale

Brushes:
nos. 2, 4, 6, 8 red sable
  brights
no. 0 red sable round

A COMMON AND CONSPICUOUS SONGBIRD, the beautiful American Robin is known and appreciated throughout all of North America. It occurs in all forest types, is a common dooryard bird, and ranks as one of the most adaptable of all our species. The Robin is a true Thrush, foraging on the ground for a wide variety of worms and insects and flocking to fruit trees as well. Named for the European Robin, which is a member of the chat-thrush family, it is similar in behavior but the birds are not closely related.

Black + Raw Umber

Black + Raw Umber + White

White + Black + Raw Umber

More White + Black + Raw Umber

Raw Sienna + White

Raw Sienna + more White (flowers)

Black + Sap Green

Sap Green + Raw Sienna + White

White + Sap Green + Raw Sienna

Raw Umber + White

Cadmium Yellow Pale + Raw Sienna

Line Drawing

This line drawing may be hand-traced or photocopied for personal use only. Enlarge at 111% to bring it up to full size. Transfer to your prepared background using dark graphite paper. Be especially careful when transferring all the detail of the eye, beak and head. The more accurate the transfer, the better the painting.

Field Sketches

American Robin on the nest photo by Terry Steele

American Robin photo by Arthur Morris

Robins readily take up residence in yards and gardens, providing exciting opportunities for even the amateur photographer. But be aware of your impact on a nesting bird; getting too close or staying too long can cause a bird to abandon the eggs or young, and your presence may even lead a predator to the nest after you leave. Here's a lovely reference photo with lots of information for painting.

In a typical foraging pose, this bird is watching and listening for any movement that will signal "lunch." When shooting reference photos of ground birds, get down on eye level as you see here. Your photos will tell a better story about the creature you're painting.

ROBIN NEST WITH YOUNG
This nest was found within a few feet of a nature center in a preserve. The mother bird would come in to care for the young even with the constant foot traffic.

Tail and Rump

PREPARE THE BACKGROUND

Base the hardboard panel, using a sponge roller, with Moss Green. Let dry, sand well. Rebase, and while wet, drizzle on a 1-inch (25mm) stripe of Desert Sun Orange and a 1-inch (25mm) stripe of Light Ivory side by side near the edge of the surface. Blend into the basecoat with the same roller, moving colors here and there primarily around the edges of the surface to distribute the color and soften into the background.

Then, in the center of the surface, drizzle 1 to 2 inches (25 to 51mm) of Flesh Tan. Blend here and there to distribute this highlight and to intermingle with the rusty tones. Let dry, sand well, and spray with Liberty Matte Finish. Refer to the Preparing the Background chapter for additional information on surface preparation.

1 **Tail:** Using a no. 4 or no. 6 bright, base dark value with Black + Raw Umber.
Rump and Back: Using the no. 4 bright, base the back with Black + Raw Umber + a little White. Add a bit more White to the mix and base the rump.
Undertail: Base with White using the no. 2.

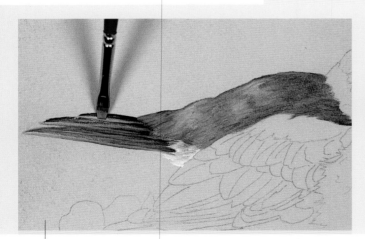

2 **Tail:** Streak feather lines with dirty brush + White.
Rump and Back: Blend where values meet, then highlight with White, applying color in several irregular patches.
Undertail: Shade with a little Raw Umber, with short choppy strokes.

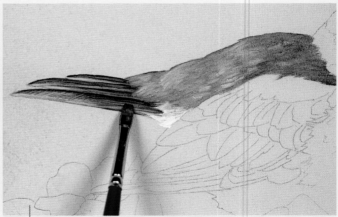

3 **Tail:** Accent with a little Burnt Sienna between some of the feather lines.
Rump and Back: Blend the first highlights with choppy strokes to give a feathery texture. Then highlight again with White. Chop final short strokes with growth direction, leaving feather texture for realistic look.
Undertail: Blend just a little between values. Connect the edge of the undertail into the bottom edge of the rump with a few choppy strokes.

Wing Feathers

1 **Primaries:** Using the no. 4, base all but the edge of each feather with Black + Raw Umber.

Secondaries: Using the no. 4, base the darker half of each feather with Black + Raw Umber. Then base the lighter half, leaving all but the edge of each feather open, using Black + Raw Umber + White.

Coverts and Scapulars: Using the no. 2, base the dark area with Black Raw Umber and the lighter value with Black + Raw Umber + White. Draw in covert feather lines with the stylus as you base over them.

2 **Primaries and Secondaries:** Fill in open edges of feathers with Raw Sienna + White, or dirty brush + White.

Coverts: Blend where the values meet, with the growth direction, within each feather. Then add feather lines with Raw Sienna + White, using the chisel edge of the no. 2 and beginning with the bottom row. As feather edge lines are completed, add central shaft lines on a few feathers with the same mix.

Scapulars: Highlight with slightly dirty White.

3 **Primaries:** At tips of primaries where the feather widens out, there's just enough room for a little lateral growth direction. Use a dry brush squeezed to a chisel edge, and pull a bit of paint from the light edge into the dark feather. Make lines close together so they form the feather fiber.

Secondaries: Do the same for the secondaries as you did for the primaries.

Coverts: Where space permits, pull a few close-together lateral feather lines from the edge of the feather inward. Where the coverts meet the bird's breast, there are two feathers that are highlighted with an area of clean White.

Scapulars: Using choppy strokes of the brush, blend the highlight. Then chop some shorter, more indistinct rows of feathers above the defined coverts to make a gradation of detail as you move up the wing.

Head and Geometrid Moth

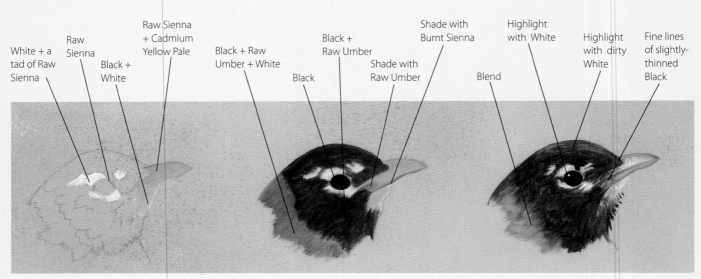

White + a tad of Raw Sienna

Raw Sienna

Black + White

Raw Sienna + Cadmium Yellow Pale

Black + Raw Umber + White

Black

Black + Raw Umber

Shade with Raw Umber

Shade with Burnt Sienna

Highlight with White

Blend

Highlight with dirty White

Fine lines of slightly-thinned Black

1. Using the no. 0 round brush, base the eye-ring with Raw Sienna. Base white markings around eye with White + a tiny bit of Raw Sienna, using the no. 0 bright. Base the beak with Raw Sienna + Cadmium Yellow Pale, using the no. 2. Base the chin with Black + White.

2. Base eye with Black using the round brush. Shade the base of beak with Raw Umber using the no. 2. Shade the under-side of the lower mandible with Burnt Sienna. Base the nape with Black + Raw Umber + White. Base rest of head with Black + Raw Umber, carefully connecting the mix to the areas around it with chisel edge zig-zags that conform to the growth direction in each area.

3. Highlight the eye with a dot of White. Highlight white eye markings with White, stippled on with flattened tip of the round brush. Blend where nape and chin meet the dark value of the head. Use a bit of the dirty White you pick up to apply a faint gray feathery highlight on top of the crown. Accent the auricular with Burnt Sienna. Blend the beak where values meet. Highlight beak with White, and stipple color a bit with flattened tip of the round brush for texture. Highlight under the chin with a little White. Finally, using the round brush and slightly-thinned Black, pull a few fine lines over base of beak.

1. Using the no. 2, base all green sections with Sap Green + Raw Sienna + White. Base sections on hindwings next to body with a mix using slightly less White. Base body with Raw Sienna.

2. Highlight wing with tiny chisel edge strokes of dirty brush + White. Stipple White highlight on body with flattened tip of the round brush.

3. Blend highlight on body with dry tip of round brush. Detail irregular section lines with tip of round brush + White. Add detail on body and do antennae with Raw Umber, slightly thinned, applied with round brush.

Breast, Belly and Phlox

1 **Breast and Belly:** Base with Burnt Sienna, following the natural growth direction as you stroke in the sparse paint, using a no. 4.

Phlox: Base with White + Raw Sienna using the no. 2 bright.

Leaves and Stems: Using the no. 4, base dark value with Black + Sap Green and Light value with Sap Green + Raw Sienna + White. Base light value of leaves at edge of design with Raw Sienna + White.

2 **Breast and Belly:** Shade with Raw Umber. Highlight with Raw Sienna + White.

Phlox: Shade with darker green mix in more shadowed areas and the lighter green mix in lighter areas. Highlight with pure White.

Leaves and Stems: Blend where values meet, following the natural growth direction of the leaves. Highlight leaves with White + Sap Green + Raw Sienna. Use the same mix to highlight down center of each stem.

3 **Breast and Belly:** Blend where values meet. Use choppy short strokes of the chisel and follow growth direction of the feathers in each area of the bird's breast and belly. Create form and shape by not overworking, retaining individual values. Think texture! Flip up a few soft feathers from breast over the edge of the wing.

Phlox: Blend where values meet, carefully following natural growth direction of each petal. With point of round brush create star-shaped center of Burnt Sienna. Fill in with a dot of White.

Leaves: Blend the leaf highlights. Add off-white flip turns with palest light green mix. Add veining with light green mix using the chisel edge of the brush. Accent with Burnt Sienna in a few shadowed areas. Blend with growth direction.

Finish: Before painting is dry, clean up any graphite lines or messy edges with the no. 8 bright dipped in odorless thinner and blotted on a paper towel.

Painted Bunting

BACKGROUND PREPARATION

Surface:
9" x 12" (23cm x 30cm)
hardboard panel, 1/8"
(3mm) thick

Delta Ceramcoat acrylic paints:
Moss Green
Tide Pool Blue
Light Ivory

FOR PROJECT

Winsor & Newton Artists' Oils:
Ivory Black
Titanium White
Raw Sienna
Raw Umber
Sap Green
Cadmium Yellow Pale
Winsor Red
Alizarin Crimson
French Ultramarine

Brushes:
nos. 2, 4, 6, 8 red sable
 brights
no. 0 red sable round

 THE SWEET SINGSONG WARBLE of the Painted Bunting is distinctive, as is the glorious red, blue, green and yellow plumage, making it the most tropical-looking of all our North American songbirds. The female Painted is a glowing spring green, our only all-green songbird, which makes her easy to identify as well. The Southeastern population of these buntings, found mainly in Florida and neighboring states, seems to be different in several ways, including timing of migration, from the Painted Buntings whose breeding range is Texas and adjacent states. Molecular studies may eventually prove these birds to be separate species.

Black + Raw Umber

Sap Green + Raw Sienna

Raw Sienna + Winsor Red

Raw Sienna + Winsor Red + White

Cadmium Yellow Pale + White

Winsor Red + French Ultramarine

Raw Sienna + White

Raw Sienna + Raw Umber

Black + French Ultramarine

Black + Sap Green

Sap Green + Raw Sienna + White

French Ultramarine + Alizarin Crimson + Raw Sienna + White

French Ultramarine + Alizarin Crimson + White

Alizarin Crimson + White

Lilac basecoat mix + White

This line drawing may be hand-traced or photocopied for personal use only. It is shown here full size. Transfer to your prepared background using dark graphite paper. Be especially careful when transferring all the detail of the eye, beak and head. The more accurate the transfer, the better the painting.

Field Sketches

Painted Bunting photo by Terry Steele

Small moths are great elements to add balance to a design: the patterns, colors and sheer abundance are remarkable. Check out a few that come to your windows at night. Scoop them up, and gently tuck them under a sheet of clear acetate on top of white paper to get some great reference photos. They can then be released unharmed to go about their lives. The moth shown here is a Noctuid.

A beautiful male Painted Bunting showing his colors just before he takes a dip in the pool. Such a photo is a wonderful reference for painting, with lots of information about colors and feather patterns.

LAZULI BUNTING
A close relative of the Painted Bunting, this species shows up for handouts in April, northbound for breeding grounds in most Western states. Sometimes the numbers are so bountiful, a quick glance makes you think that someone scattered blue pieces of paper under all the platform feeders. With luck, there's a bonus Indigo Bunting mixed in.

JUNIPER HAIRSTREAK
This tiny butterfly is common in many parts of the West. What a nice addition to a painting of a Lazuli.

Tail and Feet

PREPARE THE BACKGROUND

Base the hardboard panel, using a sponge roller, with Moss Green. Let dry. Sand well. Rebase, and while wet, drizzle on a 2-inch (51mm) stripe of Tide Pool Blue in two different places on the surface. Use the same roller to blend the blue softly here and there into the basecoat. Now add a little Light Ivory in the center of the surface, again blending and moving color around to achieve nice value gradations between the splotches of Ivory and the background. Let dry, sand well, and spray with Liberty Matte Finish. Refer to the Preparing the Background chapter for additional information on surface preparation.

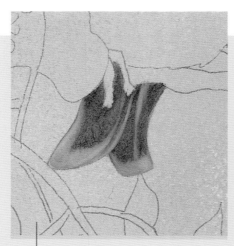

1 **Tail:** Using a no. 4 bright, base the dark value with Black + Raw Umber. Base the light value with the dirty brush + White. Let the light value feather edges be slightly widened to allow for blending.

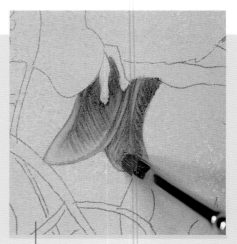

2 **Tail:** Lay in feather fiber lines with the dirty brush + White on the chisel edge of the brush following lateral growth direction. Tail tip and left side of tail should remain slightly lighter than other areas. Retouch central shaft lines with same mix.

Black + Raw Umber

Highlight with dirty brush + White

Detail lines, toenails with Black + Raw Umber

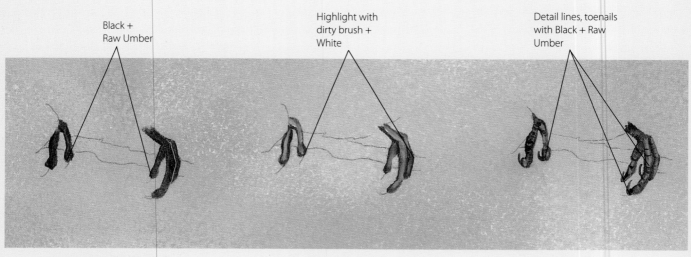

1. Base with Black + Raw Umber, using the no. 2 bright.

2. Highlight with the dirty brush + White.

3. Add detail lines on feet with Black + Raw Umber, slightly thinned, using the round brush. Do toenails with the same mix.

Wing, Belly and Breast

1 **Wing:** Using the no. 2 or 4, base the dark value with Raw Umber and the light with Sap Green + Raw Sienna.

Belly, Breast and Throat: Using the no. 4, base dark value with Raw Sienna + Winsor Red and the light central area with dirty brush + White. Even at this early stage, think about growth direction of feathers and apply paint with the correct direction to set the stage for the shape and form.

2 **Wing:** Blend where values meet. Shade with Black + Raw Umber. Highlight with Cadmium Yellow Pale + White.

Belly, Breast and Throat: Blend between values, creating a choppy, directional, feathery look. Shade with French Ultramarine. Highlight with White.

3 **Wing:** Blend where values meet, creating final direction and shape.

Belly, Breast and Throat: Blend between values once again, using choppy short strokes of the brush's chisel edge and following growth direction of the feathers to create form and shape. Let some of the light paint you carry on your brush "travel" to other areas of the breast, such as over the base of the legs, to add dimension there. Apply final White highlight if needed. Finalize the growth direction as you blend between it and the basecoat values.

4 **Belly, Breast and Throat:** When the belly and breast and throat are dry, apply a sparse bit of Winsor Red in the middle value areas and a bit of Alizarin Crimson in the darker value areas to strengthen. Use a dry no. 4 to apply paint, and blend into surface with brush or fingertip; remove any excess with a soft paper towel. Adding pure wet-on-dry accents or highlights really spark a painting that might otherwise be a bit dull.

Head and Spring Azure Butterfly

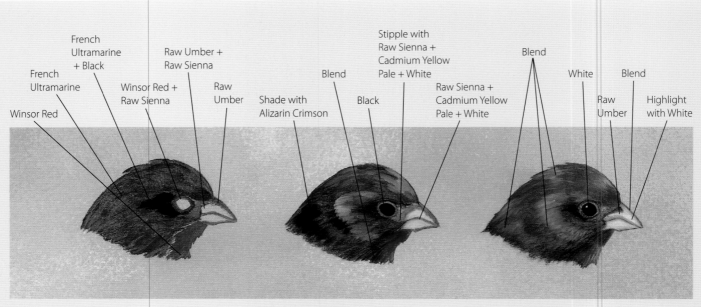

French Ultramarine

French Ultramarine + Black

Winsor Red

Winsor Red + Raw Sienna

Raw Umber + Raw Sienna

Raw Umber

Shade with Alizarin Crimson

Blend

Stipple with Raw Sienna + Cadmium Yellow Pale + White

Black

Raw Sienna + Cadmium Yellow Pale + White

Blend

White

Raw Umber

Blend

Highlight with White

1. Paint the eye-ring first, using the round brush for the eye detail. Use the no. 2 bright to paint the other head areas as shown.

2. Highlight eye-ring with Raw Sienna + White. Base eye with Black. Stipple lore with Raw Sienna + Cadmium Yellow Pale + White. Base rest of beak with Raw Sienna + Cadmium Yellow Pale + White. Blend where red throat meets blue auricular. Shade at nape with a little Alizarin Crimson. Highlight crown, forehead, auricular with White + French Ultramarine.

3. Highlight eye with White dot using round brush. Blend the beak where values meet. Stipple beak with white to highlight. Add Raw Umber nostril mark. Blend where light values meet head areas, using short strokes of the no. 2 and following growth direction carefully. Highlight throat with Raw Sienna + White.

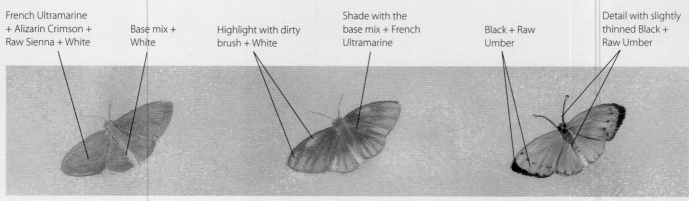

French Ultramarine + Alizarin Crimson + Raw Sienna + White

Base mix + White

Highlight with dirty brush + White

Shade with the base mix + French Ultramarine

Black + Raw Umber

Detail with slightly thinned Black + Raw Umber

1. Base the wings and thorax with a mix of French Ultramarine + Alizarin Crimson (to make a blue/violet hue) + Raw Sienna to control intensity + White to lighten, using the no. 2 bright. Base abdomen with the same mix + a little more White.

2. Shade at the base of the wings with the base mix + a bit more French Ultramarine. Highlight wings with dirty brush + White.

3. Blend where shading meets basecoat and to soften highlights. Detail margins on wings, tiny dots on wings, antennae, and spots and lines on body with slightly-thinned Black + a bit of Raw Umber using the no. 0 round.

Leaves, Stems and Lilacs

1 **Leaves:** Using a no. 4 for smaller leaves and a no. 6 for larger ones, base the dark value with Black + Sap Green. Base most of the light value area with Sap Green + Raw Sienna. In a few small areas, complete the basecoat with either French Ultramarine + Alizarin Crimson + White (violet), or the same mix with somewhat more Alizarin for a magenta hue. Blend between values with the growth direction.

Stems: Base wider stems with same green mixes used for leaves, using the no. 2. For small stems, base only with Black + Sap Green. Use same mixes and same process to do the small stems inside the lilac clusters.

2 **Leaves:** Lay in highlight areas using the light green leaf mix + more White. Blend the highlights. Add central vein structure with chisel edge, using the light value green mix. Add rolled edges with the same light value green mix.

Stems: Highlight down center of each small stem with same light value mix used for leaves. Do any final blending needed.

3 **Lilacs:** Base inside flower area, up to graphite line, with the no. 6 using a sparse mix of French Ultramarine + Alizarin Crimson + White. Vary the mix as you did for the accent basecolors on the leaves, so as to get a variation from violet to magenta. Make edges of the spike broken and ragged.

4 **Lilacs:** Overstroke with dirty brush + White using a no. 0 bright. Do not reload too frequently; let the brush run out of paint, thus giving a variation of value to the overstroked petals. Create a few "complete" florets with four strokes joining in the middle; for most, however, just do random strokes to indicate that many petals are hidden in the cluster; you want to see partial florets more often than complete ones. Accent in a few areas with Alizarin Crimson + White and with basecoat mix + more French Ultramarine, just to vary color. Highlight some petals with stronger White. Finally, dot in centers with Cadmium Yellow Pale + White using no. 0 round.

Finish: Before painting is dry, use a no. 8 bright to clean up any messy areas or graphite lines that remain visible. Dip brush into odorless thinner and blot on paper towel.

by Sherry C. Nelson

Scarlet Tanager

BACKGROUND PREPARATION

Surface:
9" x 12" (23cm x 30cm)
hardboard panel, ⅛"
(3mm) thick

*Delta Ceramcoat
acrylic paints:*
Old Parchment
Cayenne
Butter Yellow

FOR PROJECT

*Winsor & Newton
Artists' Oils:*
Ivory Black
Titanium White
Raw Sienna
Raw Umber
Burnt Sienna
Sap Green
Cadmium Yellow Pale
Winsor Red
Alizarin Crimson

Brushes:
nos. 0, 2, 4, 6, 8 red sable
  brights
no. 0 red sable round

NEVER WAS A SONGBIRD SO WELL NAMED AS THIS ONE.
Its glowing scarlet plumage contrasts so dramatically with the
black wings that once seen, it's a bird you'll never forget. In
addition, it has a lovely song as rich and bold as its plumage. And uncommonly,
even the female sings, a song that is softer and shorter than the male's, to stay
in contact while the pair is feeding or gathering nesting materials. The bird is
shown here in a branch of fruiting Biltmore Hawthorn.

Black + Raw Umber

White + Raw Sienna

White + Raw Umber
+ Black

Winsor Red + Alizarin
Crimson

Cadmium Yellow
Pale + Winsor Red

Sap Green + Black

White + Cadmium
Yellow Pale

White + Raw Sienna
+ a tad Sap Green

Line Drawing

This line drawing may be hand-traced or photocopied for personal use only. Enlarge at 118% to bring it up to full size. Transfer to your prepared background using dark graphite paper. Be especially careful when transferring all the detail of the eye, beak and head. The more accurate the transfer, the better the painting.

Field Sketches

Scarlet Tanager photo by Arthur Morris

A bird of the mixed Eastern forests, Scarlet Tanagers can sometimes be lured to yards and gardens with fruit such as oranges, banana, or suet made with peanut butter. Wouldn't it be a thrill to look in the yard and see this lovely creature?

SUMMER TANAGER
The Summer Tanager is a bird of the southern United States, with western birds being slightly larger and with bigger beaks than their eastern counterparts. It sings a complex, musical, robin-like song of three-syllable phrases.

WESTERN TANAGER
True to its name, this beautiful tanager is found in mixed woodlands in western North America. It is closely related to the Scarlet, and even their songs are similar.

Tail Feathers

PREPARE THE BACKGROUND

Base the hardboard panel, using a sponge roller, with Old Parchment. Let dry, sand well. Rebase, and while wet, drizzle on a 1-inch (25mm) line of Cayenne in two different places near the edge of the surface. Blend into the basecoat with the same roller, moving colors here and there, blending primarily around the edges of the surface to distribute the color and soften into the background.

Then, in the center of the surface, drizzle a 1- to 2-inch (25 to 51mm) line of Butter Yellow. Blend here and there to distribute this highlight and to intermingle with the rusty tones. Let dry, sand well, and spray with Liberty Matte Finish. Refer to the chapter on Preparing the Background for additional information on surface preparation.

1 **Tail:** Using a no. 4 bright, base dark value with Black + just a little Raw Umber. This complex group of tail and wing feathers takes time, and should be based with small amounts of paint, just to cover the surface but with no excess paint. That will give maximum control over the feather lines to come. Draw in feather lines with a stylus as you cover them with paint.

Primaries and Secondaries: Using the no. 4 or no. 6 bright, base each feather with Black + just a little Raw Umber. Draw in stylus lines.

2 **Tail:** Lay in feather lines with the chisel edge of the brush using Raw Sienna in areas of less light (far wing, for example) and with Raw Sienna + White where feather edges are more strongly highlighted.

Secondaries: Do the same for the secondaries as you did for the primaries.

At tips of some tail feathers, primaries or secondaries where feather widens out, there's just enough room for a little lateral growth direction. Use a dry brush squeezed to a chisel edge, and pull a bit of paint from the light edge into the dark feather. Make lines close together so they form the feather fiber.

Wings, Feet and Body

1
Coverts and Scapulars: Using the no. 2, base with Black + a little Raw Umber. Draw in covert feather lines with the stylus as you base over them.
Feet: Using the no. 2, base the toes with Black + Raw Umber.

2
Coverts: Apply feather lines with Raw Sienna + White, beginning with bottom row. As feather edge lines are completed, add central shaft lines on a few feathers with the same mix.
Scapulars: Highlight with slightly dirty White, laying on color to indicate smaller, less distinct rows of feathers.
Feet: Highlight with base mix + dirty White. Add toenails with slightly-thinned Black + Raw Umber on a round brush.

3
Coverts: Where space permits, pull a few close-together lateral feather lines from the edge of the feather inward.
Scapulars: Using choppy strokes of the no. 2, blend the highlight. Then add some shorter, more indistinct rows of feathers above the defined coverts to make a gradation of detail as you move up the wing. When wing feathers are complete, highlight some of the feathers with a light gray (base mix + White) to indicate feather sheen, mostly on the leading edge of the secondaries and the scapulars.
Feet: Detail with slightly-thinned Black + Raw Umber.
Breast, Belly and Back: Base natural shadow areas next to wing, at base of back and the mantle with Alizarin Crimson + Winsor Red. Base medium value areas with Winsor Red, and the lightest values on breast and mid-back with Winsor Red + Cadmium Yellow Pale. Follow the natural growth direction as you apply the sparse paint, using a no. 4.

4
Breast and Belly: Blend where values meet. Use short choppy strokes of the chisel and follow growth direction of the feathers in each area of the bird's breast and belly.
Flip up a few soft feathers from the breast over the edge of the wing. If you pick up a little black from the wings, do not continue to carry that color on the brush! Wipe the brush and neutralize it in a red. Wipe the brush again and continue blending. This goes a long way in preventing mud.
Apply a very slightly-thinned mix of Cadmium Yellow Pale + Winsor Red (+ a tad of White if needed) on areas to be highlighted using the no. 0 round (which prevents picking up color out of the basecoat). Then switch back to the basecoat brush and blend with the same directional, choppy stroke as before, trying not to pick up too much of the basecoat color. Keep highlights as clean as possible.

Head

1. Using the no. 0 round brush, base the eye-ring with Winsor Red. Using the no. 2, base eyeline and around base of beak with Raw Umber + Black. Base the dark value of the beak with Raw Umber + Black and the light value with dirty brush + White. Base orange areas with Winsor Red + Cadmium Yellow Pale.

2. Base eye with Black using the round brush. Blend the beak, and highlight with White. Base crown and nape with Winsor Red. Base auricular with Winsor Red + Alizarin Crimson.

3. Highlight the eye with a dot of White. Highlight eye-ring with a little White. Blend the eye-ring into the dark surrounding area. Blend the reds where values meet, following growth direction and striving for a little texture. Blend the beak highlight and add the nostril with Black + Raw Umber. Highlight the crown, forehead and auricular with Cadmium Yellow Pale + Winsor Red + a tad of White, applied with the round brush.

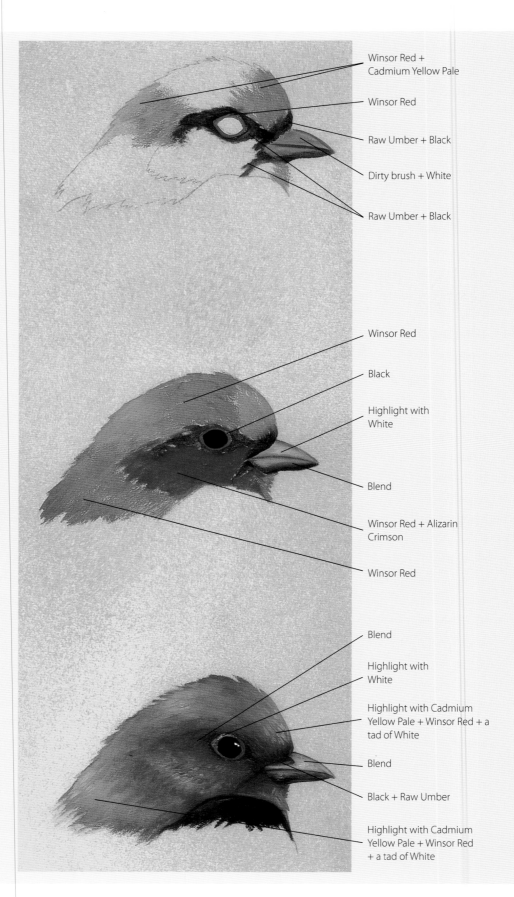

Winsor Red + Cadmium Yellow Pale

Winsor Red

Raw Umber + Black

Dirty brush + White

Raw Umber + Black

Winsor Red

Black

Highlight with White

Blend

Winsor Red + Alizarin Crimson

Winsor Red

Blend

Highlight with White

Highlight with Cadmium Yellow Pale + Winsor Red + a tad of White

Blend

Black + Raw Umber

Highlight with Cadmium Yellow Pale + Winsor Red + a tad of White

Leaves, Stems, Branch and Buds

1

Leaves: Using the no. 4 bright for smaller leaves and the no. 6 for larger ones, base the dark value with Sap Green + Black (not too blackish) and the light value with Raw Sienna + White.

Stems: Using the no. 2 or 4, base with Black + Sap Green.

Branch: Using the no. 6, base the dark value with Raw Umber and the light with the dirty brush + White.

Buds: Base with Cadmium Yellow Pale + White using the no. 0 bright.

2

Leaves: Blend where values meet, following the natural growth direction of the leaves. Highlight leaves with White + Raw Sienna. As you apply highlights, you will pick up green from the basecoat, getting a perfect mix of a very pale green.

Stems: Use the same light mix to highlight down the center of each stem.

Branch: Blend with a horizontal chisel edge, chopping in a bark-like texture.

Buds: Shade individual buds with Raw Sienna.

3

Leaves: Blend the leaf highlights. Add off-white flip turns with palest light green mix in one or two places. Add veining with light green mix using the chisel edge of the brush.

Thin a little Burnt Sienna and apply to torn edges in a few places using the round brush. Lift out a hole in a leaf or two with the damp clean-up brush and touch Burnt Sienna around it as well. Blend the edges of the blemishes with the bright brush in the growth direction.

Buds: Highlight with White and blend just a bit. Thin a little White and add tiny dabs with the round here and there.

Finish: Before painting is dry, clean up any graphite lines or messy edges with the no. 8 bright dipped in odorless thinner and blotted on a paper towel.

Evening Grosbeak Pair

BACKGROUND PREPARATION

Surface:
11" x 14" (28cm x 36cm)
hardboard panel, 1/8"
(3mm) thick

Delta Ceramcoat acrylic paints:
Trail Tan
Butter Yellow
Flesh Tan

FOR PROJECT

Winsor & Newton Artists' Oils:
Ivory Black
Titanium White
Raw Sienna
Raw Umber
Burnt Sienna
Sap Green
Cadmium Yellow Pale
Winsor Red

Brushes:
nos. 2, 4, 6, 8 red sable
   brights
no. 0 red sable round

COMMON ACROSS MOST OF THE U.S. and southern Canada, the lovely Evening Grosbeak is a beautifully-marked finch with striking white wing patches and a penchant for sunflower seeds. It has the largest beak of all our finches, and willingly comes to seed feeders in noisy flocks, especially in the winter when they return further south from their breeding grounds in Canada. Not noted for their musical skills as are the true Grosbeaks, they are nonetheless a lovely bird to have grace your yard.

Black + Raw Umber

White + Raw Sienna + Cadmium Yellow Pale

Raw Sienna + White

Burnt Sienna + Raw Sienna

Raw Sienna + White

Raw Umber + Burnt Sienna

Raw Umber + Burnt Sienna + White

Cadmium Yellow Pale + Winsor Red

Cadmium Yellow Pale + White

Raw Umber + White

Black + Raw Umber + Burnt Sienna

Black + Sap Green

Sap Green + Raw Sienna + White

Raw Sienna + Cadmium Yellow Pale

Line Drawing

This line drawing may be hand-traced or photo-copied for personal use only. Enlarge at 125% to bring it up to full size. Transfer to your prepared background using dark graphite paper. Be especially careful when transferring all the detail of the eye, beak and head. The more accurate the transfer, the better the painting.

Field Sketches

Evening Grosbeak photo by Deborah Galloway

A quick shot taken through a window of a Grosbeak poised to come to a feeder. Even a snap such as this one is good reference for size, color and pose for a species. Reference photos don't have to be of superb quality to be a great aid in your painting.

HOUSE FINCH

The female House Finch is a drab little thing, with minimal color and pattern to distinguish it. Become familiar with her, and you'll be better able to separate males and females of similar species such as Cassin's or Purple Finches as they feed together.

CASSIN'S FINCH

Here's the lovely male Cassin's Finch, characterized by a slightly crested appearance, especially when feeding with competing finches. The heavy finch-like beak marks this bird as a seed-eating species. Lucky us, we have them here at our feeders most winters.

Female Grosbeak

PREPARE THE BACKGROUND

Base the hardboard panel, using a sponge roller, with Trail Tan. Let dry, sand well. Rebase, and while wet, drizzle a 2-inch (51mm) line of Butter Yellow on the surface. Blend with the same roller to achieve good value gradations between it and the background and to distribute the yellow on the surface.

Finally, drizzle a 2-inch (51mm) line of Flesh Tan on the surface, and blend it here and there into the background using the same roller. Let dry, sand well, and spray with Liberty Matte Finish. Refer to the Preparing the Backgrounds chapter for additional information on surface preparation.

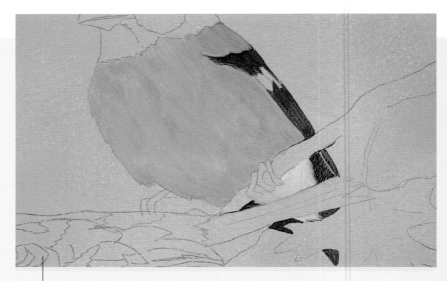

1 **Tail and Wing Feathers:** Using a no. 4 bright, base dark values with Black + Raw Umber.
Undertail Coverts: Base with White + Cadmium Yellow Pale + Raw Sienna using the no. 4.
Scapulars: Base with Raw Sienna, using a no. 2 or 4.
Breast and Belly: Using the no. 4, base with Raw Sienna in darker value areas and Raw Sienna + White in lighter central area of breast.

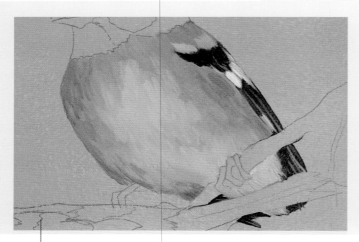

2 **Tail:** With dirty brush + White, lay in feather lines with the chisel edge of the brush, along the edges of the tail.
Undertail Coverts: Blend a little into the edge of the dark tail value below, then shade with Raw Umber.
Wing Feathers: Streak in feather lines with the dirty brush + White on the chisel edge of the brush. Base the wing patches with White.
Scapulars: Highlight with White + Cadmium Yellow Pale.
Breast and Belly: Blend with growth direction, where values meet, using short, choppy strokes of the brush. Shade with Raw Umber on flank and at edges of breast. Accent with a little Burnt Sienna on lower flank. Highlight with White + a little Cadmium Yellow Pale for a warm white.

3 **Undertail Coverts:** Blend shading a little to break hard edges of markings into the basecoat color, following the growth direction. Highlight with a bit of White if needed.
Scapulars: Blend where values meet with choppy strokes for texture.
Breast and Belly: Blend where values meet, using choppy strokes and following the growth direction. Highlight with a little more pure White, then blend a bit with growth direction to create form and shape. Accent with Cadmium Yellow Pale and soften into surrounding colors.
Feet: Base with Burnt Sienna + Raw Umber, highlight with Raw Sienna + White, and add detail lines and toenails with thinned Raw Umber.

1 **Tail, Primaries and Coverts:** Base with Black + Raw Umber on a no. 4. Draw in feather lines with a stylus as you cover them with paint.
Secondaries and Secondary Coverts: Base with White.
Undertail and Rump: Base with Cadmium Yellow Pale + Winsor Red.
Belly, Scapulars and Feet: Base with Cadmium Yellow Pale + Winsor Red. The feet are painted the same as the female's.
Mantle and Breast: Base with Black + Raw Umber + Burnt Sienna.

2 **Tail, Primaries and Coverts:** Apply feather lines with the chisel edge of the dirty brush + White. Use the no. 4 for the tail and primaries and the no. 2 for the smaller feathers.
Secondaries and Secondary Coverts: Separate feathers with streaks of Raw Umber + White.
Blend with short strokes of the chisel edge where the dark values of the mantle and breast meet the yellows of the rump and belly. Highlight the belly and rump with Cadmium Yellow Pale + White. Accent the breast with Burnt Sienna.

3 **Blend where values meet,** using choppy strokes of the brush. Make these strokes short, so they tell the story of the length of the feathers in each area. Shade undertail and outer edge of breast with a little Raw Umber, and blend where values meet. Fluff strokes of the lighter values over the top of the wing, the edge of the wing and the tops of the feet to give a natural look to the feathering.
Highlight the secondary feathers with more White. Shade below the nape on the mantle with Black + Raw Umber.

Female and Male Heads

FEMALE

1. Use the round brush for eye detail and markings; use the no. 2 bright for rest of head. Base the beak with Cadmium Yellow Pale + Winsor Red in darker areas and Raw Sienna + White in light value. Base around eye area with Raw Umber.

2. Shade between values on the beak. Highlight with White + Cadmium Yellow Pale. Base the eye with Black. Place fine eye-ring with dirty White on round brush in front and behind eye. Base the nape with Burnt Sienna + Raw Umber and next to it, a section of Cadmium Yellow Pale + Winsor Red. Base the light areas on the face with White + Cadmium Yellow Pale + Raw Sienna. Base the gray areas with Raw Umber + just a little White.

3. Blend beak where values meet, then highlight with final touch of White. Highlight eye with White. Blend the head colors where values meet, with the growth direction and short strokes of the brush's chisel edges. Shade around the beak and eye with Raw Umber. Highlight the auricular, crown and throat with choppy strokes of White.

MALE

1. Using the no. 2, base the dark on the beak with Burnt Sienna. Base outer edges with Cadmium Yellow Pale + Winsor Red. Place dark areas around eye and at base of beak with Black + Raw Umber. Dark value on crown is Burnt Sienna; light value is Cadmium Yellow Pale.

2. Base the light areas of the beak with White + Cadmium Yellow Pale + Raw Sienna. Using the round brush, base the eye-ring with a little dark mix + White. Blend where the values meet on the crown. Base the auricular and chin with Raw Umber + White.

3. Blend where values meet on beak. Highlight with a bit of White and reblend. Base eye with Black, then highlight with White, using the round brush. Highlight eyebrow and forehead with Cadmium Yellow Pale + White, and blend where values meet. Accent the chin and auricular with Burnt Sienna, and blend to soften. Base rest of head with Black + Raw Umber + Burnt Sienna. Edge into surrounding colors. Highlight behind and below eye and on auricular with dirty brush + White, chopping colors with growth direction, using short strokes of the chisel.

Oak Leaves and Acorn

1 **Leaves:** Using a no. 4 for smaller leaves and a no. 6 for larger ones, base the different hues with the following mixes. Use a little Raw Umber in some mixes, such as the gold and the green, to vary the hues.

Green Areas: Black + Sap Green.

Gold Areas: Cadmium Yellow Pale + Winsor Red.

Dark Gold Areas: Raw Sienna + Cadmium Yellow Pale.

Rust Areas: Burnt Sienna + Raw Sienna.

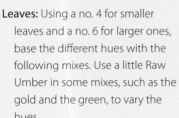

Acorn Nut: Using the no. 2, base the dark value with Black + Sap Green. Base the light value with Raw Sienna + White.

Acorn Cap: Using the no. 2, base the dark value with Raw Umber and the light value with Raw Sienna.

Branch: Base the dark value with Raw Umber and the light value with Burnt Sienna, using the no. 4.

2 **Leaves:** Blend with the growth direction, using the chisel edge of the brush. Where two different hues meet on a leaf, blend until the values connect. Lay in highlights and accents.

Green Areas: Highlight with Sap Green + Raw Sienna + White. Accent with Burnt Sienna + Raw Sienna.

Gold Areas: Highlight with Cadmium Yellow Pale + a tad of White.

Rust Areas: Highlight with Cadmium Yellow Pale.

Acorn Nut: Blend where values meet. Highlight with White.

Acorn Cap: Blend where values meet. Highlight first with Raw Sienna + White, and then White, stippling on dabs of highlight with the round brush.

Branch: Blend where the values meet, then lift out highlights within the upper half of branch with the chisel edge of the damp brush, allowing surface color to show through the branch. Re-dip the brush in thinner and re-blot when you begin carrying color.

3 **Leaves:** Reblend all highlights and accents with the growth direction, concentrating on the areas where values meet. Add the central vein structure with the damp chisel edge of the brush (dipped in odorless thinner and blotted on a paper towel) to lift out to the background.

With slightly-thinned Raw Umber, stipple in a few blemishes and bug bites here and there for a more natural look.

Acorn Nut: Blend the highlight, then accent with a speck of Raw Sienna + Burnt Sienna.

Acorn Cap: With the flattened tip of the round brush, soften the dabs of stippled highlight. Accent with just a bit of Burnt Sienna.

Finish: Before the painting is dry, clean up any graphite lines or messy edges with the no. 8 bright dipped in odorless thinner and blotted on a paper towel.

Sherry C. Nelson

Mourning Dove

BACKGROUND PREPARATION

Surface:
11" x 14" (28cm x 36cm)
hardboard panel, 1/8"
(3mm) thick

*Delta Ceramcoat
acrylic paints:*
Moss Green
Tide Pool Blue
Light Ivory

FOR PROJECT

*Winsor & Newton
Artists' Oils:*
Ivory Black
Titanium White
Raw Sienna
Raw Umber
Burnt Sienna
Sap Green
Winsor Red
Alizarin Crimson
French Ultramarine

Brushes:
nos. 0, 2, 4, 6, 8 red sable
  brights
no. 0 red sable round

THIS COMMON, SLENDER DOVE, characterized by a long tail and subtle blue-gray and tan plumage, is found in backyards across the country. It builds a casual, poorly-constructed platform nest of twigs; the eggs can often be seen through the bottom. Thankfully, their lack of architectural skill doesn't seem to hamper productivity. The mournful calls of this bird, likely responsible for its name, give a calming start to the early morning, when it's often the first bird I hear upon awakening.

Raw Umber + Raw
Sienna + White

Black + Raw Umber

White + Raw Umber
+ Raw Sienna

White + Burnt Sienna

White + French
Ultramarine

Black + Sap Green

Sap Green + Raw
Sienna + White

Previous mix + more
White

Alizarin Crimson +
French Ultramarine

White + Raw Sienna

This line drawing may be hand-traced or photocopied for personal use only. Enlarge at 111% to bring it up to full size. Transfer to your prepared background using dark graphite paper. Be especially careful when transferring all the detail of the eye, beak and head. The more accurate the transfer, the better the painting.

Field Sketches

WHITE-WINGED DOVE
Common in the southwest and in coastal areas of the east, this bird is easily distinguished by the long white wing stripe.

White-Tipped Dove photo by Terry Steele

Doves and pigeons are the only birds in North America that can drink without raising their heads to swallow!

BAND-TAILED PIGEON
This large pigeon of the western forests is difficult to see and hard to approach. We have a small flock that's gotten accustomed to us and to the seclusion of our feeders; we get great studies of this purplish dove with the striking white neck band.

WHITE-TIPPED DOVE
Larger members of this family are generally referred to as pigeons while the smaller are called doves. This White-Tipped is a south Texas bird, found in the same limited range as the Green Jay.

Tail and Rump

PREPARE THE BACKGROUND
Base the hardboard panel, using a sponge roller, with Moss Green. Let dry. Sand well. Rebase, and while wet, drizzle on a 2-inch (51mm) stripe of Tide Pool Blue in two different places on the surface. Use the same roller to blend the blue softly here and there into the basecoat. Now add a little Light Ivory in the center of the surface, again blending and moving color around to achieve nice value gradations between the splotches of Ivory and the background. Let dry, sand well, and spray with Liberty Matte Finish. Refer to the Preparing the Background chapter for additional information on surface preparation.

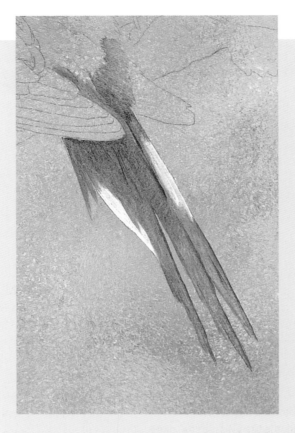

1 **Tail:** Using a no. 6 bright, base dark gray areas with Raw Umber + Raw Sienna + White. This warm gray will be used in various values throughout the piece and will be referred to as the "Gray Mix."

Rump: Using the no. 4, base with Raw Umber + Raw Sienna + a bit more White than for tail.

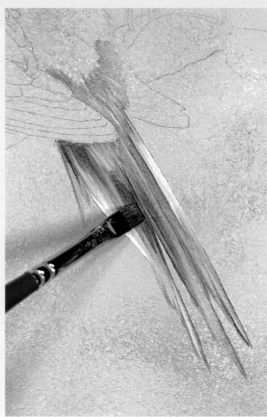

2 **Tail:** Blend the rump color over the top of the tail with fluffy strokes. Shade darkest areas with Black + Raw Umber. Highlight the edges of white feathers with more White, and pull dirty brush + White lines from the tip of the tail upward into some of the narrow feathers to indicate feather shaft lines, or highlights.

Rump: With White on a no. 4, highlight the rump feathers with short strokes, and fluff some additional White under the wing tip to suggest rump feathering that continues under the wing feathers.

1 **Primaries:** Base with Black + Raw Umber using the no. 4 bright. Draw feather lines into the wet paint with a stylus as you cover them.

Secondaries, Coverts and Scapulars: Base with the Gray Mix, using the no. 2 for smaller feathers and the no. 4 for larger ones. Draw the feather lines back into the wet paint as you cover them, using the stylus.

Dark spots: Base with the no. 2 using Black + Raw Umber.

Back and Mantle: With a no. 4, base the dark areas with Raw Umber and the light areas with the Gray Mix + a little more White.

Belly: Base with White, using the no. 4.

Breast: Base the dark value with Raw Umber and the light value with the Gray Mix + a little more White.

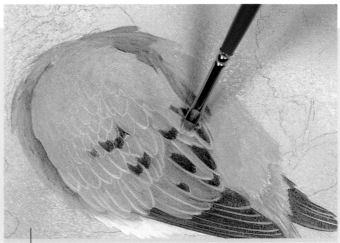

2 **Primaries:** Streak in feather lines using the chisel edge of the dirty brush + White.

Secondaries and Coverts: Streak in feather lines using the dirty brush + White.

3 **Scapulars:** Chop in short feather markings using French Ultramarine + White.

Back and Mantle: Blend where values meet. Highlight with White. Use choppy short strokes of the chisel and follow growth direction of the feathers to create form and shape.

Breast and Belly: Blend between values, creating a choppy, directional, feathery look. Highlight with White.

4 **Scapulars:** Blend feather strokes to soften. Fluff a few strokes over the coverts to give a fluffy appearance. Brush in sparse Burnt Sienna to accent.

Back and Mantle: Blend with short, choppy strokes of the chisel edge to soften highlights and to finalize their direction. Note the unusual growth direction of feathers above the wing, on the mantle and back. Slice in a few dark lines with Raw Umber to suggest shadows underneath feather layers and allow the lights to be strongest on top, helping to give form and shape to the bird. Add a bit of sparse Burnt Sienna for accent.

Breast and Belly: Blend with short, choppy strokes of the chisel at the edges of highlight values, gradually creating a final value gradation. Be cautious with growth direction. Accent with sparse Burnt Sienna.

Head and Feet

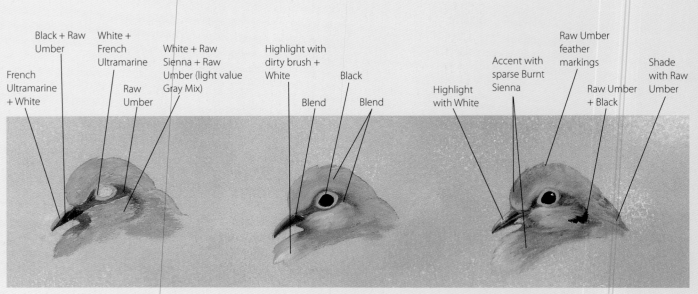

French Ultramarine + White

Black + Raw Umber

White + French Ultramarine

Raw Umber

White + Raw Sienna + Raw Umber (light value Gray Mix)

Highlight with dirty brush + White

Blend

Black

Blend

Highlight with White

Accent with sparse Burnt Sienna

Raw Umber feather markings

Raw Umber + Black

Shade with Raw Umber

1. Paint the eye-ring first, using the round brush for the eye detail. Use the no. 2 bright to paint the other head areas as shown.

2. Base eye with Black. Blend where values meet on beak. Blend where values on head meet. Highlight on cheek and upper breast with dirty brush + White.

3. Highlight eye with White dot using round brush. Blend the beak where values meet. Rehighlight beak with White if needed. Blend the highlights on upper breast and auricular with growth direction, using short strokes of the no. 2. Shade at the nape with Raw Umber. With the little Raw Umber remaining on the brush, add some faint feather markings on crown. Add facial marking with Raw Umber + Black, using the round brush. Add a very sparse amount of Burnt Sienna accent on forehead and below auricular. Highlight forehead and crown with White + a bit of French Ultramarine + a bit of Sap Green. Highlight at nape with Raw Sienna first, then Raw Sienna + White.

1. Base with Burnt Sienna using the no. 2 bright.

2. Accent with a bit of sparse Winsor Red, then highlight with dirty brush + White.

3. Add detail lines on with Raw Umber, slightly thinned, using the round brush. Do toenails with slightly-thinned Raw Umber + Black. Highlight toenails with White.

1

Leaves: Use a no. 4 for smaller leaves and a no. 6 for larger ones. Base the dark value with Black + Sap Green. Base light value edges with Sap Green + Raw Sienna + White or French Ultramarine + White.

Stems: Base wider stems with same mixes used for leaves on a no. 2. Base small stems with Black + Sap Green.

Branch: Base dark value with Raw Umber and light value with dirty brush + White on a no. 6. Apply paint sparsely and in broken patches.

Berries: Vary application so berries of the same color aren't grouped. Use a no. 2 to basecoat.

Purple berries: Base dark value with Alizarin Crimson + French Ultramarine. Base light value with Alizarin Crimson.

Red berries: Base dark value with Alizarin Crimson; medium value with Winsor Red; light value with Sap Green + Raw Sienna + White.

Red/green berries: Base dark value with Winsor Red; light value with the green mix.

Green berries: Base dark value with Sap Green + Raw Sienna + White. Base light value with same mix + more White.

2

Leaves: Blend between values, with the growth direction, using the chisel edge of the brush. Lay in highlight areas using the light value mixes + more White. Pull a central vein with light green mix.

Stems: Highlight down the center of each small stem with the same light value mix used for the leaves.

Branch: Blend where values meet to create a bark-like texture. With Raw Umber, shade in stronger shadow areas.

Berries: Blend between values using the no. 2. Using the no. 0 bright, or the flattened tip of the round brush, apply small strokes of Raw Sienna + White in the center of each round segment.

3

Leaves: Blend the highlights. Add the final central vein structure with the chisel edge, using the light value green mix.

Stems: Do any final blending needed.

Branch: Blend the Raw Umber shading color to soften. Add any additional highlights desired with White, and blend those.

Berries: Using the no. 0 bright, blend around the edges of each tiny highlight stroke to create a value gradation that will give roundness to each segment. When all blending is done on a berry, roll the tip of the round brush into pure White and add a dot of White in several of the most dominant segments.

Finish: Before the painting is dry, clean up any graphite lines or messy edges with the no. 8 bright dipped in odorless thinner and blotted on a paper towel.

Western Meadowlark

BACKGROUND PREPARATION

Surface:
11" x 14" (28cm x 36cm) hardboard panel, 1/8" (3mm) thick

Delta Ceramcoat acrylic paints:
Trail Tan
Butter Yellow
Flesh Tan

FOR PROJECT

Winsor & Newton Artists' Oils:
Ivory Black
Titanium White
Raw Sienna
Raw Umber
Burnt Sienna
Sap Green
Cadmium Yellow Pale
Winsor Red
Alizarin Crimson

Brushes:
nos. 0, 2, 4, 6, 8 red sable brights
nos. 0 and 1 red sable rounds

 MEADOWLARKS HAVE DISTINCTIVE AND PLEASING SONGS, and in fact, the vocalization is the most reliable way to tell the Eastern Meadowlark from the Western. In several states the ranges overlap, so becoming familiar with the melodies of these very similar species is the quickest way to distinguish them. Meadowlarks are members of the Icterid family, which also includes Blackbirds and Orioles.

Raw Umber + White

White + Raw Umber

Cadmium Yellow Pale + Raw Sienna

Previous mix + White

Black + Raw Umber

Raw Sienna + Burnt Sienna

Previous mix + White

Black + Sap Green

Sap Green + Raw Sienna + White

Cadmium Yellow Pale + Winsor Red

Raw Sienna + Raw Umber

Winsor Red + Burnt Sienna

White + Cadmium Yellow Pale

Cadmium Yellow Pale + a little Winsor Red + Raw Sienna + White

Sap Green + Raw Umber

This line drawing may be hand-traced or photocopied for personal use only. Enlarge at 111% to bring it up to full size. Transfer to your prepared background using dark graphite paper. Be especially careful when transferring all the detail of the eye, beak and head. The more accurate the transfer, the better the painting.

Field Sketches

Western Meadowlark photo by Terry Steele

An excellent diagnostic look at a Western. The throat and the malar are brilliant yellow, distinguishing it from the Eastern. And teed up on this bush, he's likely going to sing as well, verifying our identification.

EASTERN MEADOWLARK
Only the throat on this species is yellow. The malar may be pure white or a value of gray. Meadowlarks can open their beaks with great strength. Thus they have evolved an unusual feeding technique called "gaping" in which they insert the closed beak into dirt or grasses and then open it to pull apart the substrate, peering in to find exposed food items. This technique is also used by other members of the family, and may help account for the Icterids' continued success despite dramatic habitat loss.

WESTERN MEADOWLARK
Note the entirely yellow throat and malar.

Tail, Wing and Body

PREPARE THE BACKGROUND

Base the hardboard panel, using a sponge roller, with Trail Tan. Let dry, sand well. Rebase, and while wet, drizzle a 2-inch (51mm) line of Butter Yellow on the surface. Blend with the same roller to achieve good value gradations between it and the background and to distribute the yellow on the surface. Drizzle a 2-inch (51mm) line of Flesh Tan on the surface and blend it here and there into the background using the same roller. Let dry, sand well, and spray with Liberty Matte Finish. Refer to the chapter on Preparing the Background for more information on surface preparation.

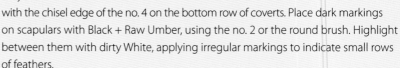

1

Tail: Using a no. 4 bright, base dark outer feathers with Raw Umber + White. Base rest of tail with White + Raw Umber. Shade along edges with Black.

Primaries: Base with Raw Umber using the no. 4 bright. Draw in feather lines with stylus if desired, then apply feather lines with dirty White on the chisel edge of the brush.

Wing Coverts and Scapulars: Base around the markings with White + Raw Umber, using the no. 2. Apply dirty brush + White feather lines with the chisel edge of the no. 4 on the bottom row of coverts. Place dark markings on scapulars with Black + Raw Umber, using the no. 2 or the round brush. Highlight between them with dirty White, applying irregular markings to indicate small rows of feathers.

Breast and Belly: Using the no. 4, base the dark area with Raw Umber + a little White, and the medium value with Cadmium Yellow Pale + Raw Sienna. Base light area with White, carefully avoiding covering the markings in the white flank area. Blend between breast and flank and between the Raw Umber shading and the yellow breast, to create a value gradation, following the natural growth direction and using short choppy strokes of the brush's chisel edge. Highlight with dirty White + Cadmium Yellow Pale. Lay in the Raw Umber markings on the flank area using the no. 2.

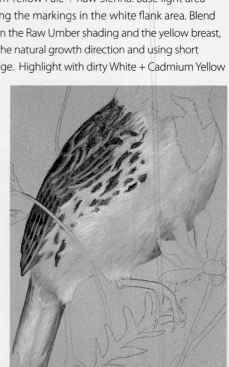

2

Tail: Use a little White on the brush to blend the two sections of the tail with the growth direction.

Primaries, Wing Coverts and Scapulars: Add additional dark detail markings with slightly-thinned Black + Raw Umber, using the round brush. Highlight a few feather edges with cleaner White if they become gray, using the no. 2.

Breast and Belly: Blend the highlights, following growth direction and using short strokes, being careful to avoid markings. Rehighlight with more White if desired.

Markings: Define more carefully with Black + Raw Umber, using the no. 2 or the round. Do not allow dark mix to blend into the basecolor. If you begin carrying color, stop, wipe the brush, and reload before continuing.

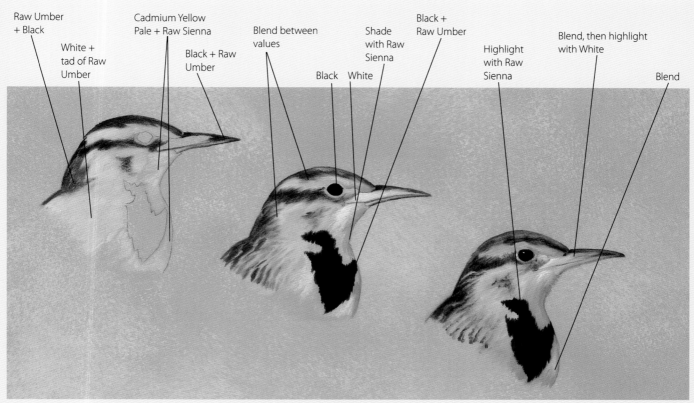

Raw Umber
+ Black

White +
tad of Raw
Umber

Cadmium Yellow
Pale + Raw Sienna

Black + Raw
Umber

Blend between
values

Shade
with Raw
Sienna

Black +
Raw Umber

Black   White

Highlight
with Raw
Sienna

Blend, then highlight
with White

Blend

1. Paint the eye-ring with White + Raw Umber on no. 0 round. Base nape, top of crown and beak, and eyeline with Black + Raw Umber on a no. 2 bright. Base white areas with White + Raw Umber. Base throat, breast and lore with Cadmium Yellow Pale + Raw Sienna.

2. Base eye with Black. Blend between crown, nape and eyeline values with growth direction with very short strokes. Do not overwork. Highlight crown with dirty White. Base light value of beak with White. Shade yellow breast area, throat and lore with Raw Sienna. Highlight side of throat, breast and lore with White. Base black breast area with Black + Raw Umber. Place detail markings first with Raw Umber and then strengthen with Raw Umber + Black in darkest areas, using the no. 2 or no. 0 bright.

3. Highlight eye with White dot using round brush. Blend the beak where values meet. Rehighlight beak with White if needed. Highlight eyebrow and wider portion of eye-ring behind and under eye with White. Blend shading and highlights on throat, breast and lore, following growth direction and using very short strokes. Highlight black breast area with Raw Sienna. Retouch the detail markings if needed.

Forewing: Base the darker value with Cadmium Yellow Pale + Winsor Red. Base the lighter value with dirty brush + Raw Sienna + White, using the no. 2.

Hindwing: Base with dirty brush + Raw Sienna + White, using the no. 2.

Body: Base with Raw Sienna + White.

Forewing: Shade the orange area with Winsor Red. Highlight with White + Raw Sienna. Detail the wing margin with White + Raw Sienna, using no. 1 round brush.

Hindwing: Detail margin with White + Raw Sienna on round brush.

Body: Stipple with White + Raw Sienna on round brush.

Forewing: Detail with slightly-thinned Black + Raw Umber on the round brush.

Hindwing: Detail with slightly-thinned Raw Sienna + Raw Umber.

Body: Shade with Raw Umber, using the no. 0 bright. Detail legs, eye and antennae with slightly-thinned Raw Umber on the no. 0 round brush.

1 **Leaves:** Using a no. 4, base the dark value with Black + Sap Green. Base light value areas with Sap Green + Raw Sienna + White.

Stems and Calyxes: Base the stems and calyxes with Black + Sap Green, using the no. 2 or no. 4.

Blanket Flower Petals: Base with Cadmium Yellow Pale + Winsor Red, using the no. 2.

Centers: Base with Raw Sienna + Raw Umber, using the no. 2.

Feet and Legs: Base the bird's feet and legs with Raw Sienna + Burnt Sienna on a no. 2; highlight with the dirty brush + White. Add detail lines with slightly thinned Raw Umber on a round brush. Highlight toenails with a bit of dirty White.

2 **Leaves:** Blend between values, with the growth direction, using the chisel edge of the brush. Lay in highlight areas using the light value mix + more White.

Stems and Calyxes: Highlight down center of each small stem with same light value mix used for leaves. Highlight calyxes with same mix.

Petals: Shade with Winsor Red + Burnt Sienna at base of each petal. Highlight with White + Cadmium Yellow Pale on overlapping petals and at outer tips.

Centers: Shade with Raw Umber using choppy strokes of the no. 0 bright. Highlight with Raw Sienna + White, using the tip of the no. 1 round brush.

3 **Leaves:** Blend the highlights. Add the central vein structure with the brush's chisel edge, using the light value green mix. Accent with Raw Sienna on some leaves and Burnt Sienna on others. Blend to soften.

Stems and Calyxes: Blend as needed.

Petals: Blend the shading where values meet, following growth direction of petals. Blend highlighting to follow growth direction as well, but try to retain a yellow area in between the dark and light values. Detail petals with fine lines of slightly-thinned Alizarin Crimson, using the round brush.

Centers: Highlight as needed.

Finish: Before painting is dry, clean up any graphite lines or messy edges with the no. 8 bright dipped in odorless thinner and blotted on a paper towel.

Green Body Areas: Base with Sap Green + Raw Umber using the no. 0 bright.

Wing: Base the dark value with Raw Umber and the light value with White + Raw Sienna, using the no. 0 bright.

Head: Base with Raw Sienna using the no. 0 bright.

Green Body Areas: Highlight with the green base mix + White.

Wing: Highlight with dirty brush + White.

Head: Highlight eye with dirty White.

Green Body Areas: Detail with lines of Raw Umber, using the round brush.

Wing: Streak wing with fine lines of White, using the round brush.

Legs and Antennae: Detail with slightly-thinned Raw Umber. Highlight legs with dirty White.